Ukrainians in Michigan

DISCOVERING THE PEOPLES OF MICHIGAN

Russell M. Magnaghi, *Series Editor*
Arthur W. Helweg and Linwood H. Cousins, *Founding Editors*

Ethnicity in Michigan: Issues and People
Jack Glazier and Arthur W. Helweg

Discovering the Peoples of Michigan is a series of publications examining the state's rich multicultural heritage. The series makes available an interesting, affordable, and varied collection of books that enables students and educated lay readers to explore Michigan's ethnic dynamics. A knowledge of the state's rapidly changing multicultural history has far-reaching implications for human relations, education, public policy, and planning. We believe that Discovering the Peoples of Michigan will enhance understanding of the unique contributions that diverse and often unrecognized communities have made to Michigan's history and culture.

Ukrainians in Michigan

Paul M. Hedeen and Maryna Hedeen

Michigan State University Press

East Lansing

♾ The paper used in this publication meets the minimum requirements
of ANSI/NISO z39.48-1992 (R 1997) (Permanence of Paper).

Michigan State University Press
East Lansing, Michigan 48823-5245

LIBRARY OF CONGRESS CATALOGING-IN-PUBLICATION DATA
Names: Hedeen, Paul M., 1953– author. | Hedeen, Maryna, author.
Title: Ukrainians in Michigan / Paul M. Hedeen and Maryna Hedeen.
Description: East Lansing : Michigan State University Press, [2023] |
Series: Discovering the peoples of Michigan |
Includes bibliographical references and index.
Identifiers: LCCN 2022014574 | ISBN 978-1-61186-447-2 (paperback) |
ISBN 978-1-60917-717-1 (PDF) | ISBN 978-1-62895-484-5 (ePub) |
ISBN 978-1-62896-478-3 (Kindle)
Subjects: LCSH: Ukrainians—Michigan—History. |
Ukrainian Americans—Michigan—History. |
Ukrainian Americans—Michigan—Social life and customs. |
Ukraine—Emigration and immigration—History. |
Michigan—Emigration and immigration—History. |
Immigrants—Michigan—Social conditions.
Classification: LCC F575.U5 H43 2023 | DDC 977.4004/91791—dc23/eng/20220525
LC record available at https://lccn.loc.gov/2022014574

Cover photo: Echoes of Ukraine Dance Troupe, circa 1970.
Courtesy of Ukrainian American Archives and Museum.
Cropped and recolored to grayscale. Used with permission.

Visit Michigan State University Press at *www.msupress.org*

Contents

Introduction

I n 1885 Mykola Stefansky entered Detroit's already established, thriving, and transitioning economic center. Having left Western Ukraine in 1882 for the Pennsylvania coal mining region, he came to Detroit's German community accompanied by his wife and three children. There Stefansky worked in a wire plant before opening a tavern. The Stefansky family met two other Ukrainians, "a Kmitzinsky and Yash," and formed the nucleus of what would become an eight-family cluster in the Livernois–Michigan Avenue neighborhood.[1] At least on record, these families were the first of what would become a vibrant and growing Ukrainian immigrant presence not only in Detroit, but also in small clusters across Michigan.[2]

Because there are as many Ukrainian immigrant histories as Ukrainian immigrants, generalizations regarding their resettlement in Michigan are both problematic and necessary, whether we view a Ukrainian's choice of destinations as either the humanist's hero's journey; the social scientist's response to significant economic, military, or political pressures; or both.[3] In the Ukrainian diaspora—whether in the United States, Canada, Europe, or South America—there is always this tension between individual and collective choice. Succinctly stated, understanding a Ukrainian's immigrant experience means understanding both the hero, the special risk-taker open to adventure and opportunity, and (in the same era) a frightened people who have been pressured or coerced, victims rather than heroes, "huddled masses yearning to breathe free."[4] Following established networks, Ukrainians were called to Michigan by the need for cheap, adaptable, and hardworking laborers. Ultimately, they thrived in Michigan's mining, forest, agricultural, manufacturing, and intellectual communities.

As this book will describe, the Ukrainian immigrant's choice to move to Michigan—whether in the nineteenth, twentieth, or twenty-first centuries—has been encouraged by both Ukraine's complex geographical, economic, and historical circumstances and Michigan's special opportunities. Michigan's Ukrainians came in four waves, each unique in time and character. As Myron Kuropas states, "Each immigrant wave left a different Ukraine and arrived in a different America," making precise descriptions about cause and effect very difficult.[5] Adding to this difficulty was the U.S. Immigration Service, for the agency waited "until the 1990s . . . [to list] immigrants from Ukraine . . . as 'Ukrainian.'"[6] This oversight is replicated in other important scholarship and, therefore, is difficult to redress.[7] In the end, Michigan's Ukrainian immigrants' estimable success and prosperity have relied upon their ability (and luck) to fit into what David Gerber refers to as Michigan's "opportunity structure," that evolving, regional matrix of cultural and economic needs new arrivals, as assets, were required to meet.[8] The circumstances of Ukrainian emigration and the immigrants' ability to meet the needs of Michigan's opportunity structure are the subjects of this book.

Ukrainians in Michigan will begin by introducing the geographical and historical contexts underlying a Ukrainian's choice to emigrate from the "old country" of Ukraine to Michigan. Chapter One will then describe the specific circumstances of "the four waves" of Michigan's Ukrainian immigrants. The Ukrainian participation wave by wave in Detroit's opportunity structure will be discussed in Chapter Two, and the Ukrainians' greater presence in Michigan "beyond metro-Detroit" will be surveyed in Chapter Three. Chapter Four will highlight the cultural practices of Michigan's Ukrainians, while Chapter Five will offer thirteen brief biographies of prominent Ukrainian-Michiganders belonging to the various immigrant waves.

CHAPTER ONE

The Old Country

U kraine is an independent European nation geographically situated to share borders with seven other Western, Central, and Eastern European countries: the Russian Federation, Poland, Belarus, Slovakia, Hungary, Romania, and Moldova. Before World War I, Ukraine existed tenuously as a nation between empires—chiefly the empires of Poland, Austro-Hungary, and Imperial Russia. To a significant degree, Ukraine was controlled, manipulated, and exploited by these empires. Ukraine's name, which is commonly translated as "borderland," was, therefore, apt.[1]

Being the target of its neighbors has contributed to the ethnic and cultural diversity of Ukraine, for wherever it has shared a border, it has been influenced by the other country's people and customs. Ukraine, however, is not an amalgam or vassal state without its own unique culture, as the now obsolete habit of referring to the nation regionally as "the Ukraine" would suggest.[2] Despite the political and cultural imperialism of its neighbors, Ukraine (population approximately forty-two million) is home to an advanced, sophisticated, and fiercely independent people.

With a land mass larger than both France and Spain, Ukraine is second only to the Russian Federation when the overall area of European countries is compared. Were it not populated as it is and possessing of its massive size, Ukraine would not have survived centuries of its neighbors' envy and

Ukraine and its neighbors (COURTESY OF THE NATIONS ONLINE PROJECT. CROPPED AND RECOLORED TO GRAYSCALE. USED WITH PERMISSION.)

hegemony. Ukraine's unstable political history, physical location as a borderland, and coveted mineral wealth and agricultural fertility have often contributed to a hard life for its population. Ukrainians have often felt compelled to emigrate to countries promising more independence and economic opportunity. Since the last quarter of the nineteenth century, a destination for wave upon wave of Ukrainians has been North America, both Canada and the United States. Within the United States, the state of Michigan has become the home for a significant number.

The Four Waves of Immigration: The First Wave

Immigration from the old country of Ukraine was pursued by individuals and family groups during all periods of American history. Beginning in the late nineteenth century, the destinations of this immigration included the already booming region of southeast Michigan. While experts Orest Subtelny and Myron Kuropas both refer to those "picturesque forerunners" who made the hero's journey and appear in history's annals as early as the Jamestown colony, both recognize Michigan's Ukrainians were part of a predominant

Table 1. Top Five European Countries Ranked by Area			
RANK/COUNTRY	**SQ. KM**	**SQ. MILES**	**NOTES**
1. Russia	3,972,400	1,533,800	17,098,242 km² (6,601,668 sq mi) including Siberia
2. Ukraine	603,628	233,062	Includes territory illegally occupied by Russia
3. France	551,695	213,011	643,801 km² (248,573 sq mi) when the overseas departments are included.
4. Spain	498,511	192,476	505,990 km² (195,360 sq mi) when the Canary Islands, Ceuta, and Melilla are included
5. Sweden	450,295	173,860	

Ukrainian immigration to the United States that occurred in three waves.[3] Recent scholarship adds a fourth wave, and it is possible that the Russian Federation's 2022 invasion of sovereign Ukraine will add a fifth. The first wave was the largest, longest, and most impactful and accordingly will receive the most attention here.

As Michigan's first recorded Ukrainians, Mykola Stefansky and his family were in the first wave of Ukrainian immigration to North America. This wave began in the last quarter of the nineteenth century and persisted until World War I (1870–1914), and, as Subtelny adds, was "composed mostly of hardworking peasants—young single men predominated . . . [from the] Transcarpathia and the Lemko regions, the westernmost and least developed of Ukrainian lands." Rumors about the United States, "the semi-mythical land far across the sea," where an enterprising young man (echoing a trope of the hero's journey) might earn, according to Subtelny, "ten to twenty times as much as at home," had been spread east from other countries in the Austro-Hungarian empire. What became an exodus from Western Ukraine, however, required opportunity structures, most real but some imaginary. Only these structures would beckon the adventurous and the desperate.

Those heeding this call came in 1877 when "a Pennsylvania coal company, confronted by a strike, decided to bring in cheap labor."[4] "Network lines" began to be established by the company's agents.[5] They "offered young . . . Transcarpathians money for the journey—to be deducted later from their earnings." Smoldering interest was fanned to flame by news and money spread around by returnees from the United States. Lengthy and uncomfortable wagon and train rides took eager young men across borders and through many document checks "to reach the major ports of embarkation," which included Bremen, Hamburg, Antwerp, Rotterdam, and Trieste.[6]

Knowing something about the history of Western Ukraine and the conditions persisting there helps explain why first-wave immigrants were so tempted. Western Ukraine is not the storied "bread basket" region of Ukraine so prized by Western Europe and Russia. Those fertile and vast steppes of wheat, sugar beets, and sunflowers belong to Central and Eastern Ukraine, which had been dominated in the eighteenth and nineteenth centuries by Imperial Russia. Rather, Western Ukraine consists of Galicia, Bukovyna, and Transcarpathia, regions that were part of the Austro-Hungarian empire, but were dominated during the nineteenth century, according to Subtelny, "by powerful, local élites." Galicia (West and East Galicia) was dominated by Polish nobles, Bukovyna by Romanians, and Transcarpathia by Hungarians. In each of these provinces, the Ukrainians primarily were rural peasantry. Creating an advanced economy to compete with Bohemia, Lower Austria, and Moravia, however, wasn't in the landowning élites' interest or to their advantage. To do so would siphon off the cheap available labor serving their estates. As summarized by Subtelny, the provinces of Western Ukraine "remained an agrarian society, with little capital accumulation, weak internal trade, low urbanization, minimal industry, and the lowest wages and highest labour surplus in the empire."[7]

Sought-after land reforms came with the disabling requirement that the peasantry assume the debt accompanying land transfers from nobles to the peasants. Impoverished by the very changes meant to empower them, Western Ukrainians, far from inhabiting vibrant and developing parts of the Austro-Hungarian empire, were laboring at almost subsistence levels in marginalized and exploited ethnic enclaves. Moreover, from 1849 to 1910, there was a fifty-four percent population growth. As farms in hilly and mountainous regions were further subdivided to accompany the increased numbers of sons, the economic situation only worsened as the nineteenth century gave way to the twentieth.

Overtaxed farms of ever-decreasing size, low wages on landowner estates, little access to capital, and, correspondingly, increasing malnutrition, famine, and disease meant that "at the turn of the [twentieth] century the life span of the West Ukrainian male was six years less than that of a Czech and thirteen years less than that of an Englishman."[8] The childhood (age five and below) mortality rate was fifty percent and alcoholism—encouraged by landowners who produced the alcohol and tavern keepers who exchanged wage chits to sell it—became a significant health hazard.[9] The intense attachment many Ukrainians had to their small strips of land would not survive their dour realization that to stay meant abject poverty and an early death.

Still, the attachments were strong, and testing them could be a source of great stress and sorrow. As attested to by both Ukrainian literature and folk music, emigration was not embarked upon without trepidation, sadness, and loss. In a widely read short story, "Kaminny Khrest" (Stone Cross), author Vasyl Stefannyk describes a poor Ukrainian family that decides to immigrate to the United States. The story focuses on the sufferings of the father who joins his adult children in their search for a better life overseas. All his life, this old man had only a small piece of land that was uphill and so rocky that it was almost impossible to farm. He spent years walking uphill and downhill hauling rocks and trying to improve the quality of the soil. He ruined his health and became obsessed with this rocky strip of land. When asked to leave everything for the unknown United States, he decides to make a stone cross on the top of his rocky hill. The main character collects rocks and carries them uphill to make a cross for himself. After he has finished his own grave marker, he throws a combination farewell party and funeral dinner. He drinks to his friends and relatives asking for forgiveness and explaining to them that he will die at some time after leaving his homestead. He knows that he will die among strangers, and there might be neither a cross nor memorial service for him. He also feels that leaving his home and place where his ancestors lived is a kind of death. The stone cross is his attempt to take care of all his earthly business, so whatever happens overseas will not really matter. This short story is required reading in Ukraine's literature curriculum. It is masterfully written and expresses the plethora of emotions, fears, and fatalism of many older immigrants who came to the United States in the first wave.

Folk songs also make immigration their subject. One widely sung folk song of that time is "Hamerytsky Kraj" ("Land of America"). It is a monologue of a person who lives in Transcarpathia and is thinking about leaving for the United States. He looks around and understands he cannot leave his beloved mountains and river. He decides that it is easier to be poor at home than to live as a stranger in an unknown land.[10] These two popular examples help illustrate that immigration was not viewed innocently as a guarantee of success.

Ukrainians who were preparing to leave for the United States were very worried about their lives because often they had to sell everything to be able to leave. Much was unknown. Even though Ukrainian Americans wrote to their families from the United States, the letters from those who struggled were not very informative. People tried hard to read between the lines as they decided whether they should make the journey. Those who did were often sorry. Exploited, cheated, and crammed into substandard accommodations, Western Ukrainians made their way to Ellis Island in New York Harbor for processing and for further exposure to charlatans and opportunists. This meant that the average immigrant might have been "robbed by fake travel agents, defrauded by unscrupulous emigration officials, exploited by steamship companies, and misled by industrial recruiters."[11] Surviving this passage, bureaucratic processing in ports of exit and entry, and what often amounted to outright fleecing, most Transcarpathian immigrants (followed by those from the Lemko region and Galicia) were not encouraged to resume the agrarian lives of their peasant past but were coerced to take on the hazardous, oppressive, and regimented lives of coal miners and factory workers.[12] Some Ukrainians had to walk from New York to Pennsylvania and sleep outdoors, for locals frequently weren't willing to mix with "colorful" and "curious" foreigners who spoke no English.[13]

Uninformed and misunderstanding the situation, Ukrainians often "went to work as strike-breakers; consequently they brought upon themselves the hatred of old miners, mostly Irishmen."[14] Assaults, riots, and "accidents" in the mines, some producing injuries, some ending in death, were not uncommon.[15] Ukrainians, through no desire of their own, therefore, "tended to keep the wages low, and this prolonged the racial and labor antagonism" between newcomers from Ukraine (and the rest of Eastern Europe) and established Western and Northern European miners who were attempting to unionize.[16] Ukrainian miners soon worked in every major mine in Pennsylvania and took up coal and other forms of mining almost everywhere work was available: West Virginia, Ohio, Texas, the Dakotas, Minnesota, Colorado, and Michigan.[17] Once established, some miners (like Mykola Stefansky) left the mining towns and moved to cities for factory work and saloonkeeping.

There were, of course, exceptions to the mines, foundries, mills, and fabricating plants. For some, savings created opportunities to purchase small farms.[18] Pockets of homesteaders found their way to Virginia and the Dakotas, while individuals scattered almost anywhere land remained unclaimed.[19] For most first-wave Ukrainians, however, the opportunity structure of unspecialized manual labor could be thus summarized:

> Since specialized skills were not a necessity, Eastern Europe's millions of excess workers fit the bill perfectly. Available, mobile, and plentiful, they arrived unencumbered by families. Moreover, they were more tractable than the unionized German, Scottish, and Irish workers. Steamship companies cooperated with coal-mining concerns by directing the flow of East Europeans to Pennsylvania . . . the steel mills of Ohio, located in Cleveland, Youngstown, and Akron . . . [and] the big cities . . . [of] New York, Philadelphia, Chicago, and Detroit.[20]

Established networking ensured that "before the First World War, 98 per cent of Ukrainians lived in the northeast and well over 70 per cent were concentrated in Pennsylvania."[21] Many first-wave Ukrainian immigrant men had no intention of staying and were working to acquire the money needed for a better life back in the old country. Most, however, "eventually stayed in the United States. They married immigrant women or sent home for wives and fiancées to join them and set up house in America."[22] But theirs was not an easy life. Back-breaking unskilled work for non-union pay, poor living conditions, exploitative child labor, and little hope for full citizenship were, at first, their lot. Dr. Osyp Krawczeniuk describes the plight of first-wave, stateless Ukrainians:

Illiterate and lacking knowledge of the English language, our immigrants
patiently endured cruelty and abuse . . . Toughened by hard work in their
native land, they did not fear dangerous work in mines . . . [T]hey toiled
endless hours cracking the hard rock in the dark underground. Without
doubt among all the immigrants, these people [Ukrainians] endured the
greatest misfortunes. Other nationality immigrants received care and aid
from home countries; their priests, teachers and other professionals came
with them . . . to organize a religious, cultural and economic life . . . Our
people were without their own state and government. Among them there
were no educated leaders and, more importantly, there weren't any priests
to whom they could look for direction. . . . [T]hey had no Ukrainian church
in their new homeland.[23]

There was at first very little family life, which would become necessary to
sustain parish life. Contrary to the popular stereotype of the multigenera-
tional household, most of the first-wave Ukrainian immigrants were men.
Subtelny notes that "even as late as 1905, only one of three Ukrainian immigrants was a female."[24] Interestingly, unlike many of their male counterparts,
Ukrainian women tended not to repatriate, so the ratio increased to one of
two.[25] As the numbers of women increased, they found employment as domestics and workers in "light industry, especially factories manufacturing
cigarettes, cigars, textiles, and clothing" for wages "much lower than those
of the men."[26] Because they were at first far outnumbered, Ukrainian women
typically did not remain unmarried. Some worked in the same factories as
their husbands, doing lighter work, for shorter hours, and (as noted) lower
pay.[27] Because of their own preferences and predilections, not to mention
their relative affordability, many Ukrainian women worked as domestics in
other people's homes and in cities for agencies cleaning larger buildings and
facilities.[28] In mining towns and rented company homes, Ukrainian women
were often severely tasked with not only large households but also six to
twelve boarders who also required food and laundry services. The hours
were ones "of continuous toil and hardship."[29] The women's days were not
better around pay times, for the money earned by boarders brought "days of
drunkenness, singing, arguments, and occasional fighting."[30]

Eventually, like other national groups in their mining towns and
city neighborhoods (Russians, Poles, Slovaks, Bohemians, Lithuanians,

Germans, and the Irish), Ukrainians found fellow immigrants with whom they shared linguistic and cultural identity. In Michigan, they eventually networked and established families, Ukrainian Catholic and Orthodox parishes, schools, reading rooms, cultural centers, youth assemblies, mutual aid societies, workers homes, art and publishing concerns, and political interest groups. A complex acculturation process ensued in which immigrants, themselves immersed in a new culture, passed along the old ways to their children. Remembering his father Michael (a second-wave Ukrainian immigrant to Michigan), Stephen Wichar explains,

> Sometimes sociologists call my generation cultural hybrids . . . persons living and sharing in the cultural life and traditions of [multiple] peoples . . . and we have been identified with the land of our birth [Ukraine] and its institutions. Despite this, in the process of [the immigrant children's] learning the mother tongue, the standards of morals and religion, sentiments and patterns of foreign thoughts through such media as Ukrainian schools, dancing groups, stage and other folklore, the [simultaneous] assimilation [into both old and new countries] has been successfully possible for many of us.[31]

It is perhaps needless to say that Ukrainian and other Eastern European communities in Michigan, as elsewhere, endured hostility from the largely assimilated, established, and preferred Anglo-Saxon, Western, and Northern European communities making up the American "melting pot." This hostility grew from more than labor competition in the mines, as social ills like poverty, vice, "liquor smuggling and anarchist radicalism" were attached to ungoverned immigration from Windsor, Canada.[32] As the first-wave Ukrainians were largely illiterate, poor, and vulnerable, established immigrant-rivals fell back on well-learned Western and Northern European ethnocentric notions regarding racial difference and raised suspicions that Slavs and other groups were racially inferior to them. Anyone establishing new network lines could be a target. Ashley Bavery summarizes,

> The rapid growth of the automobile industry brought thousands of newcomers to the city, prompting Detroit's established [and favored] residents to demand immigration laws aimed at closing the border. In the 1910s and 1920s southern and eastern European, Arab, Mexican, and African

American migration changed the ethnic and racial makeup of the city. Once
new migrants reached Detroit, they found jobs, established neighborhoods,
and . . . organized politically. . . . These changes incited a nativist backlash
from groups like the Ku Klux Klan and the Daughters of the American Revolution, whose members sought to close the border and restrict immigration
from groups they saw as undesirable.[33]

Nativism appealed mostly to economically vulnerable working-class
whites whose labor competed directly with the immigrants. Disturbances in
1919 seemed to corroborate sensational nativistic paranoia when a wave of
anarchist bombings accompanied the growing unionism of Italian, Finnish,
and Ukrainian communists. Foreign leftists protested their working conditions, compensation, and union recognition and contributed to the staging
of more than forty strikes in Detroit alone.[34]

Following the example of other growing Eastern European groups,
Ukrainians developed self-protective tendencies when confronted with
nativistic discrimination and prejudice, establishing neighborhood clusters
around Ukrainian Catholic and Orthodox parishes and their own mutual aid
societies, workers' homes, and financial institutions. First-wave Ukrainian
assimilation and prosperity in Michigan would take multiple generations of
vigilance and hard work before the burdens of nativistic race- and class-cen-
tered bias could be lessened.[35] Given the politics of the nineteenth century
and an already robust gender discrimination, Ukrainian women had to labor
in an even more oppressive environment than the men. Single women or
widows could be easily exploited, and independent living was for all practical
purposes impossible. Marriage was the pathway not only to companionship
and family life, but also to social and economic stability.

The Second Wave

The second wave of Ukrainian immigration, roughly spanning the years
between the World Wars (1920–1939), was marked by stressed and broken
network lines, changed immigrant motivations, and evolving opportunity
structures. Radicalization of liberal and socialistic elements in all of Europe
and the hyperviolence and unrest attending this radicalization helped
increase, in the more conservative United States, the already active nativistic xenophobia toward immigrants generally and Eastern Europeans

specifically. Fear and prejudice provided the political impetus to modify government immigration statutes, which disrupted first-wave network lines. First came the Immigration Act of February 5, 1917, which expanded the definitions and descriptions of deportable aliens. Then congress passed the Act of May 22, 1918, which assigned to the President the responsibilities to monitor and control departure and entry during wartime and national emergencies.[36] At least in Detroit, such laws created new network lines by escalating illegal river crossings from Canada. Bavery describes the nativists' backlash and the industrialists' adjustment to their opportunity structures:

> The new federal immigration laws of the 1920s prompted a rise in smuggling, but in Detroit, a key site of illegal immigration, employers, immigrants, smugglers, and federal enforcers determined the consequences of new laws. In 1921, responding to Nativist lobbies set in place by local chapters of the Ku Klux Klan and patriotic societies, Congress . . . established permanent quotas for immigrants from southern and eastern Europe . . . But despite the federal legislation, automobile companies resented the restrictions on their labor. To ensure that the Detroit-Windsor border would continue a long-standing tradition of open trade and border crossing, major employers established branch plants in Windsor and, in some cases, disregarded new laws altogether by employing smuggled immigrants in their factories . . . By the mid-1920s, immigrant smuggling became a major underground industry in the Detroit-Windsor region.[37]

The Quota Law of May 19, 1921, referred to in the preceding quote from Bavery, established quantitative limits of three percent of the foreign-born of any nationality already in the United States (by 1910). This meant, of course, that more established and assimilated—not to mention racially, politically, and religiously correct (Protestant)—groups from Anglo-Saxon countries, Northern Europe, and Western Europe would sustain their privileges. Exemptions were granted only to those who had maintained one year of continuous residency in a Western European country. The cap on immigration was 350,000. The Act of May 11, 1922, extended the act of May 19, 1921, by two years and increased the residency requirement for exempted applicants to five years in a Western European country, thereby denying immigration to those who were using Western Europe as a "stopover." A subsequent act, the Immigration Act of May 26, 1924, increased restrictions within its quota system by overtly and more specifically targeting *national* groups and resetting the cap to two percent of the number of American foreign-born persons of any nationality while pushing the determining date back to 1890. The overall cap from all nations was lowered to 164,667. Adjustments to the determining date (1920) and caps—ensuring that no national origin number or percentage exceeded a percentage of 150,000 overall (in short, a cap on a cap)—made the policy even more restrictive. Quota laws were largely in place until the Refugee Relief Act of August 7, 1953, and the Nationality Act Amendments of October 3, 1965.[38]

Immigrants in Canada, however, could simply hire a smuggler to get them across the largely unguarded and unpoliced frontier, thereby sidestepping any quota. Windsor and Detroit for many years enjoyed an alternative network line between ethnic communities on both sides of the Detroit River. This line created a rise in "smuggling, policing, and deportation [which] gave nativists who had long practiced grassroots harassment a legal outlet for their xenophobic ideas."[39] Nativist groups, Bavery writes,

> like the Ku Klux Klan and the Daughters of the American Revolution (DAR), which had traditionally favored mob violence and letter-writing campaigns, respectively, began to condemn immigrants with a new label: "illegal immigrants." Soon smugglers, their immigrant clients, and even the inhabitants of ethnic neighborhoods across the city [of Detroit] came to be indiscriminately associated with criminality.[40]

If "illegals" obscured the true totals of Ukrainian immigration during the second wave, so, too, did the new legislation. Because Ukraine was a nation for only two years (1919-1920) during the interwar, second-wave period, and a politically divided nation at that, nationality quota systems meant that a Ukrainian (Ruthenian) immigrant could have been considered a representative of any of several Central and Eastern European nationalities (all of them restricted): a former citizen of Austria, Hungary, Romania, Poland, or the USSR. The USSR eventually eliminated legal westward immigration almost completely. So, for approximately two decades, wars, revolutions, border and regime changes, and increasingly restrictive legal immigration policies slowed legal (tallied) immigration to the United States. While the first wave of large-scale Ukrainian immigration (1870-1914) numbered approximately 554,000, with significant numbers settling in Michigan, the second-wave immigration (1920–1939) was limited to only 15,000 to 20,000.[41] The Canadian situation was slightly better, but there, "poor economic conditions in the farming regions and more restrictive [Canadian] immigration policies limited the number of new Ukrainian arrivals to 70,000."[42] How many of this total stayed in Canada and how many became "ghost walkers" between Windsor and Detroit are impossible to know.[43]

While nativistic pressures restricted immigration on this side of the Atlantic, Europe's travails energized the need for immigration and changed the motivation of a potential immigrant. These travails, which included the reassertion of imperial domination in 1919, this time via Czarists, Bolsheviks, and the resurgent Poles, meant Simon Petlura's free Ukraine would not survive past 1920.[44] Post-World War I treaties (1919–1923) sponsored by the United States and Western Europe ended the fighting by awarding parts of Western Ukraine to a reformed Poland, Romania, and Czechoslovakia. Central and Eastern Ukraine was claimed by an increasingly autocratic and repressive Bolshevik-dominated USSR, which severely limited emigration.

As World War I brought down the great empires of Europe (Austro-Hungarian, German, and Russian), the possibility of independence and freedom energized the political aspirations of many Eastern Europeans, including Ukrainians. Ukraine's unsuccessful bid for independence and subsequent repartitioning by its neighbors (as just described) created immigrants who might be better labeled as political émigrés. Subtelny writes,

> After the defeat of the various Ukrainian governments in the 1917-20 period, tens of thousands of their supporters—soldiers, officers, government functionaries, and many members of the nationally conscious intelligentsia, together with their families—followed them [the governments] into exile . . . The desire to help Ukraine achieve independence remained for these veterans an overriding concern.[45]

Fleeing the chaotic end of World War I and its cataclysmic changes (1920), second-wave immigrants became the politically active faction of what has come to be called the Ukrainian Diaspora. While Ukrainians have always been interested in preserving their cultural and linguistic uniqueness, many second-wave immigrants brought with them the active fractiousness and divisiveness characteristic of modern Ukrainian history and politics. Subtelny writes, "Even those whose motivations for leaving were primarily economic

had been exposed . . . to the fierce conflicts that wracked their homeland
. . . and were . . . more sensitive to political issues than the earlier wave"
of Ukrainians.[46] Moreover, while first-wave Ukrainians assimilated their
political interests with the U.S. political processes and parties, second-wave
Ukrainians expressed, according to Subtelny, "the exclusive, even obsessive,
orientation towards Ukraine."[47]

While it would be a mistake to draw too fine a line or make strict cat-
egorical distinctions (after all, human nature was not dependent upon being
first- or second-wave), a real generational difference had emerged, one that
would account for very different immigrants with a strikingly different way
of expressing their nationality. First-wave immigrants' economic survival
depended less upon consciousness of the "old country" and more upon assimilation with and adaptability to what was dominantly "American." They
contrasted and sometimes competed with second-wave immigrants, whose
political understandings and Ukrainian identities had been shaped less by
economic necessity and more by the dislocations and traumata of revolution, war, and failed independence.

From 1921 to 1923, the Bolsheviks for the first time used starvation as a
form of social and political control, using drought as an opportunity to create an artificial famine.[48] Under Joseph Stalin, the USSR explored ways to
suppress Ukrainian nationalism and any ethnic sense of uniqueness and
economic independence: "In 1932 Stalin decided to vanquish the Ukrainian
farmers by means of starvation and thus break the Ukrainian national revival
that had begun in the 1920s and was rekindling Ukrainian aspirations for an
independent state."[49] After closing Central and Eastern Ukraine to outsiders
and preventing emigration, the Soviet program of collectivization, forced
compliance, and blacklists was introduced, a program that destroyed private
agriculture. With their own financial system in default, the Soviets began to
leverage Ukrainian agricultural products for foreign trade. The levies upon
and outright confiscation of Ukrainian agriculture impoverished the coun-
tryside and resulted in what has come to be called the Holodomor, in which
seven million Ukrainians died of starvation.[50] The USSR complemented the
starvation with an active repression called The Great Terror, a process at
multiple locations in Central and Eastern Ukraine of arrest and execution of
tens of thousands of Ukrainians considered politically unreliable.[51] Outright

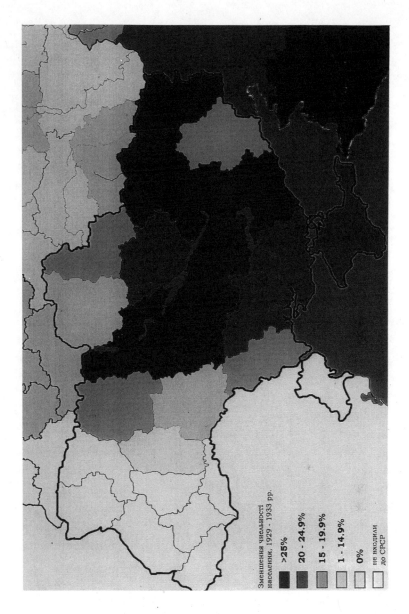

Famine map. Losses in population from Holodomor in Soviet Ukraine as percentage of population. Western provinces at this time belonged to Poland, Hungary, and Romania. (COURTESY OF SERGENTO. CROPPED AND RECOLORED TO GRAYSCALE. USED WITH PERMISSION.)

murder and internal exile further reduced the Ukrainian population by 200,000 and four million people, respectively.[52]

With national instability and powerlessness, a brutal World War, violent revolution, changing geopolitical masters, and outright terroristic starvation and political murder as a backdrop, second-wave immigrants were energized by dynamic senses of victimization and patriotism not shared with first-wave immigrants. As subsequent chapters regarding Detroit and the rest of Michigan show, both groups had their gifts and influences. First-wave immigrants to Michigan knew how to assimilate with the opportunity structures they had joined. They laid the foundation, culturally and economically, of Ukrainian immigrant life in the United States. Ukrainian culture was important, but only tangential to their lives as Americans. According to Subtelny, second-wave immigrants, "because there were many educated, talented, and committed individuals in their ranks . . . had much to contribute to the Ukrainian communities in the New World."[53] These interwar Ukrainian immigrants—"professionals, intellectuals, military officers, and religious leaders, as well as members of the [Austro-Hungarian or Russian] empire's former aristocracy"—established an "Age of Ideological Commitment" in Michigan's Ukrainian communities by creating homeward-looking political organizations, variously socialistic, communistic, monarchical, Hetmanite, and nationalistic.[54] Nationalistic groups were more in keeping with nativist America's overriding conservative ideology and were the most successful at finding a following. Moreover, nationalism "called for the creation of a new type of Ukrainian, one who was unconditionally committed to his nation and to independent statehood . . . [via a] mythologized Ukrainian history, which emphasized the cult of struggle, of sacrifice, and of national heroes."[55] When the rush of ongoing lives in a progressive new culture helped memories of the real Ukraine to fade, these second-wave Ukrainians' commitment "focused increasingly on an abstract, ideologized notion of their homeland. Thus, Ukrainianism became increasingly intermeshed with ideology."[56] It is clear that this radicalized and (dare we say) idealized Ukrainianism, like parishes and priests for first-wave Ukrainians, also faded as the inevitable forces of assimilation worked upon the United States-born children of second-wave immigrants. As noted by Subtelny,

> Acceptance of American . . . ways usually meant rejection of things Ukrainian. Proficiency in English was accompanied by a growing disinclination

to use Ukrainian. As Ukrainian language use declined among the young, so too did their access to the cultural traditions of their parents.[57]

This attenuation of home-country ties was not unique to Ukrainians but was a typical experience among older members of other immigrant ethnic groups. In the half century or so since the beginning of the first wave, then, both network lines and the immigrant pool itself had been altered. Network lines had been transformed in the United States by nativistic pressures on immigration legislation and in Europe by the collapse of empires. In addition, second-wave Ukrainian immigrants were linguistically more sophisticated, internationally competent, and professionally diverse. Fewer of them went to the Pennsylvania coal fields or prairie farms. Most joined, legally and illegally, the children of the first-wave immigrants in large cities promising diverse access to the American economy. While first-wave immigrants had tended to remain in the careers and neighborhoods that welcomed them, their children, grandchildren, and second-wave immigrants were bolder, variously and extensively educated, and more thoroughly indoctrinated in American progressiveness. According to Subtelny, the new second-wave immigrants sought to make both horizontal and vertical movements in the economy:

> Whereas among the pre-1914 immigrants there had been one or two doctors or lawyers, there were dozens in the interwar generation. In a field like engineering, where there were no Ukrainians before the First World War, there were over a hundred after. Teaching was an especially popular profession.[58]

The Third Wave

While first-wave Ukrainian immigrants to Michigan could be considered economic opportunists and those of the second wave political émigrés, third-wave immigrants (1948–1955), mostly those who came from displaced persons camps in Western Europe, are best described as war refugees.[59] Seeing immigrants as refugees requires revisiting World War II's impact upon Ukraine, something about which most Americans still know very little. The Ukraine that displaced persons left *during* World War II in significant ways ceased to exist *after* World War II. Moreover, involvement in Western Europe during the war—whether this involvement was voluntary (as a guest worker), coerced by a labor-hungry Germany, or inspired by Ukrainian nationalism and its hatred of Russian Communism—usually meant a Ukrainian returnee would serve time in the Gulag labor camp system or, if he or she had been a fascist soldier, would be shot outright. However, once again, there were regional differences in history and fate.

Ukraine's midcentury travails, however, began at World War II's outset. As noted in discussions of first- and second-wave immigrants, Western Ukraine was administrated separately and regionally by Poland, Hungary, and Romania, with Central and Eastern Ukraine dominated by the USSR—that is, until the Molotov–Ribbentrop pact, signed on August 23, 1939. A BBC article explains its importance:

> Officially it was a non-aggression, neutrality pact [between the USSR and Nazi Germany]. But under a secret protocol agreed to in Moscow by the countries' two foreign ministers, Latvia, Estonia and Finland were to be consigned to the Soviet sphere while Lithuania came a few days later. Poland was to be carved up and part of Romania handed to the Soviets.[60]

A prelude to the "carving" was the German invasion of Poland on September 1, 1939, which invoked the secret protocol allowing the USSR to dominate and annex eastern Poland, supposedly in support of Belarus's and Ukraine's Soviet puppet regimes. Poland was about equally divided between Germany and the USSR, both in land mass and in population. Western Poland, of course, would go to Germany. As Eastern Poland went, so did Western Ukraine, which meant that for the first time all of Ukraine was in Russian control. This first Russian occupation, however, was short-lived, for on June 21, 1941, Germany disastrously broke its non-aggression pact, invaded the USSR, and sent its southern army group into Ukraine. What followed was more than three years (1941–1944) of violence and suffering. Politically, the catastrophe of the German occupation began with Germany breaking its promise of independence. Maria Savchyn Pyskir, an early Galician recruit to the OUN, the Ukrainian Nationalist Home Army and Government, remembers her nascent, naive joy:

> In the first days of July, a poster appeared in the village that announced the formation in Lviv of a government headed by Stepan Bandera's OUN faction. The poster said that Bandera had promulgated an act of Ukrainian independence on June 30, 1941. . . . It was hard to believe that

suddenly Ukraine was a sovereign nation. How quickly and easily it had happened.[61]

Believing that the enemies (the Germans) of their enemies (the Russians) were their friends, Ukrainian nationalists at first sided with the invading Nazis. Pyskir's mother was not as easily duped, advising her daughter not to be "'so glad about the arrival of Germans. Do you think Hitler sent his armies because he wanted us to be rid of the Bolshevik yoke? Think again . . . He wants to rob and enslave us.'"[62] Confirming the mother's dire prediction in mere days, the invading Nazis arrested Bandera and other OUN organizers and placed them in concentration camps and began Germany's administration of what was to be an exploited colony of slaves. Galicia was returned to Poland (already part of the German Reich) and the rest of southwest Ukraine became the province of Transnistria, which was given to Romania.[63] As it was freed from Soviet occupation, the bulk of Ukraine was administrated directly by Germany. In one short year, this administration's policies of oppression and outright murder were in full view of Pyskir and her OUN comrades:

> Gestapo pressure and terrorism of the population was [sic] becoming increasingly brutal. Jews had been rounded up and taken away to concentration camps. Political activists faced sudden arrest, while young, able-bodied men and women were seized and forced onto trains that took them to labor camps in Germany. Every day the population was subjected to senseless brutalities.[64]

The Nazis had already begun to implement their racial policies by this time. Christopher R. Browning documents "the murderous swath Police Battalions 45 and 314 cut across" Soviet Ukraine in the fall of 1941 (as Pyskir's mother had suggested):

> Police Battalion 45 had reached the Ukrainian town of Shepetovka on July 24 . . . Within days the battalion had massacred the several hundred remaining Jews of Shepetovka, including women and children. Three-figure massacres in various Ukrainian towns followed in August. In September the battalion provided cordon, escort, and shooters for the execution of thousands of Jews in Berdichev and Vinnitsa. The battalion's brutal activities climaxed in Kiev on September 29 and 30, when the policemen again provided cordon, escort, and shooters for the murder of over 33,000 Jews in the ravine of Babi Yar.[65]

Repeated and uncounted mass killings of Ukrainian Jews and partisans continued until the Germans were defeated and expelled in 1944. As noted by Timothy Snyder, the German murder of Ukrainians was part of the German policy and plan for Eastern Europe:

> The Holocaust overshadows German plans that envisioned even more killing. Hitler wanted not only to eradicate the Jews; he wanted also to destroy Poland and the Soviet Union as states, exterminate their ruling classes, and kill tens of millions of Slavs (Russians, Ukrainians, Belarusians, Poles). If the German war against the USSR had gone as planned, thirty million civilians would have been starved in its first winter, and tens of millions more expelled, killed, assimilated, or enslaved thereafter. Though these plans were never realized, they supplied the moral premises of German occupation policy in the East.[66]

Envisioning aside, what the Germans did accomplish was terrible enough. And to understand the human cost of this terror—in short, to see it through eyes of a Slavic internee in a displaced persons camp in 1945 as he or she contemplated returning home—we need to consider the whole of this internee's memory of war as a *culmination* of violent ideologies and policies practiced by both a vanquished Germany and a triumphant USSR. This memory begins in the 1930s as fascists and communists maneuvered for and consolidated power and then for four terrible years exerted this power over people more or less powerless. Snyder summarizes,

> In the middle of Europe in the middle of the twentieth century, the Nazi and Soviet regimes murdered some fourteen million people. The place where all of the victims died . . . extends from central Poland to western Russia, through Ukraine, Belarus, and the Baltic States. During the consolidation of National Socialism and Stalinism (1933–1938), the joint German-Soviet occupation of Poland (1939–1941), and then the German-Soviet war (1941–1945), mass violence of a sort never before seen in history was visited upon this region . . . [T]hese people were all victims of murderous policy . . . [N]ot a single one of the fourteen million murdered was a soldier on active duty. Most were women, children, and the aged.[67]

The human cost, as horrific as it was, does not constitute the entire cost, which requires the addition of material losses. For more than three years

German and Soviet armies fought over the whole length of Ukraine.[68] The net effect of World War II's material destruction in Ukraine was summarized by Kuropas: "By October 1944, Ukraine was back under Stalin's control. But Ukraine was in ruins. The conflict had destroyed more than 700 Ukrainian cities and 28,000 villages."[69] With the whole of devastated Ukraine now controlled by the Russians, Russification, collectivization, Stalinist repression, state terror, suppression of the Ukrainian church, and famine returned. This resurgent Soviet violence-by-policy, the memory of the fourteen million, and the continued violent Ukrainian nationalism are the backdrop to the emigration decisions of third-wave Ukrainians (many of whom were Christians, nationalists, or both) still interned in Western Europe.

This backdrop came to include the gradually increasing tensions between the USSR and its former allies in the West. Eventually, this so-called Cold War would hamper further emigration from much of Central Europe and all of Eastern Europe. Polish, Belarusian, Baltic, and Ukrainian internees—avoiding postwar Soviet persecution, wartime destruction, probable imprisonment, certain poverty, and ongoing starvation—looked to the United States, South America, the Commonwealth, and Western Europe for an opportunity to avoid the fate of their relatives subsisting on the scorched earth of what used to be the old country but was now a "bloodland."

The displaced persons' first opportunities were in Western Europe itself, South America, and the Commonwealth countries. However, with the Displaced Persons Act of June 25, 1948, the possibility of finding a new home in the United States became a reality.[70] Initially, 205,000 war refugees were covered by the 1948 act. This number was later increased to 315,000, and the augmenting Refugee Relief Act of August 7, 1953, added 214,000 more visas.[71] Ukrainians took advantage of this liberalization. Of the hundreds of thousands of refugees allowed in by the United States, approximately 85,000 were Ukrainian nationals.[72]

These third-wave Ukrainians differed significantly from earlier Ukrainian immigrants. Emigration had never been their intent. The war had been a disruption of well-planned and, for some, privileged lives. Simply speaking, third-wavers had been caught up in a war not of their choosing. For the most part, they were motivated by fear of persecution, extreme need, and ideology. Most were stridently anti-communistic and nationalistic. They were better educated and included higher percentages of "college graduates and professional people such as doctors, lawyers, and college professors."[73] Frequently, they had a more cosmopolitan outlook than their predecessors, had traveled well beyond village and region, and knew languages other than Ukrainian and Russian. Network lines with the well-established Ukrainian-American community offered assistance, sponsorship, and a refined sense of a Ukrainian immigrant's role in contemporary America. Moreover, unlike first- and second-wave immigrants from rural western Ukraine, many third-wave immigrants came from cities and were comfortable in and adaptable to postwar urban opportunity structures. Many had been successful in Ukraine and expected to be successful in the United States. They joined American institutions and organizations and made cultural, political, and economic contributions early rather than late. They believed strongly in fully educating their children. While all these traits made third-wavers assimilable, these traits also made them competitive in the higher levels of employment, which created suspicion and resentment among more established immigrants and citizens.[74]

The Fourth Wave

Since 1991, the year of the collapse of the USSR and Ukraine's independence, there has been a fourth wave of immigration.[75] The UAPOST.US summarizes the situation in this way:

> Even before the Soviet Union collapsed . . . [Ukraine's] economic indexes were dwindling, but the industry decay accelerated during the 1990s. The prosperity was not achieved regardless of the western aid and opening of markets. By most measures of economic and social well-being, Ukraine's post-independence performance has been extremely weak as unemployment has risen and legal wages have fallen. As such, it is little surprise that this tumultuous transition to capitalism has produced yet another wave of migration . . . Between 1992 and 1997, a total of 107,916, or an annual average of 18,000 people who had been born in Ukraine immigrated legally to the US . . . As a result, the US is now home to one of the largest Ukrainian diasporas. As of 2009, we stand 976,000 strong (US Census Bureau, 2011). Unofficial records suggest this number may be closer to 2.5 million individuals.[76]

Table 2. Four Waves of Ukrainian Immigration to the United States		
WAVE	DATE	APPROX. TOTAL
1	1870–1914	554,000
2	1920–1939	20,000
3	1948–1955	85,000
4	1992–1997	108,000

This fourth-wave immigration (1991–present day) is hardly surprising, given the improved opportunity structure of the U.S. economy, competitive wages, affordable transportation, freedom of movement, and supportive network lines reaching back over a century through three previous waves of immigration. Contemporary travel hardships are virtually nonexistent, for immigrants can arrive in less than a day by air. Generally, only visa regulations have controlled the flow of individuals from the former republics of the USSR. Fourth-wave immigrants are well educated, career focused, internationally aware, and linguistically sophisticated. They assimilate quickly into the professions.

Late Fourth-Wave (Recent) Immigration

Recent immigration includes many contemporary Ukrainians who do not see themselves as part of a Ukrainian diaspora. They are not economically powerless and tractable, willing to work even as a strikebreaker in a coal mine or on the assembly line in Highland Park to gain wealth, like first-wave immigrants. They are not politically disenfranchised and yearning for freedom, like second-wavers. Nor are many refugees, like third-wavers, fleeing a "bloodland" or the USSR's active suppression, persecution, and war.[77] Like fourth-wave Ukrainian immigrants generally, late fourth-wavers are a diverse group of people mostly seeking increased socioeconomic and educational benefits in the United States. These immigrants speak Russian, Ukrainian, and English. Those who prefer Russian often socialize with other Russian-speaking immigrants from former USSR republics. Often these people have had similar experiences in their childhood and youth. They meet from time to time to share their favorite foods and jokes, reflect on their old and new lives, and discuss the peculiarities of being an immigrant in the United States. They tend to have special gatherings around major secular holidays in Ukraine, such as New Year's Eve, International Women's Day (March 8), and Labor Day (May 1).

Michigan's late fourth-wave Ukrainian immigrants can be classified according to their religious affiliation. Many are Christians who attended Eastern Orthodox churches in the homeland (Ukrainian Orthodox church, Ukrainian Catholic church, or Russian Orthodox church). Reflecting Poland's influence on contemporary Ukraine, some may have attended Ukraine's Latin Rite Catholic churches. There are also significant numbers who attended different Protestant churches. The last group includes Ukrainians who never attended any church in Ukraine and do not associate themselves with any particular branch of Christianity.

Of all these groups, Ukrainians who attended Eastern Orthodox and Latin Rite Catholic churches will care most strongly about and strive to preserve their national heritage. Ukrainian-speaking and bilingual (Ukrainian and Russian speaking) immigrants often join orthodox Ukrainian parishes and participate in their activities. If a Ukrainian immigrant marries a non-Ukrainian speaker, a family might switch to English-speaking sermons at Ukrainian churches or to non-Ukrainian English-speaking churches. If a family of Ukrainian-speaking parents has children and wants to involve them in the Ukrainian community, it can send the children to Ukrainian schools, heritage schools, and youth organizations. This is particularly true of those immigrants who live close to Ukrainian parishes. It is important to note that many immigrants choose traditions over religion, cooking traditional foods and wearing national costumes for Christmas and Easter, even if they are not religious. Favoring national culture over religious observation is common in contemporary Ukraine as well.

As mentioned earlier in this chapter, the Russian Federation's vicious and unprovoked 2022 invasion of independent and sovereign Ukraine may create out of the millions of temporary refugees to Poland, Germany, Hungary, Moldova, and Romania a fifth wave of immigrants to the United States. Like the war refugees of the third wave, many of them may be allowed to follow the network lines of the past and settle in Michigan.

CHAPTER TWO

Ukrainians in Detroit

Michigan drew much interest from Ukrainian immigrants in all four (and the late fourth) waves, and they live in all of Michigan's regions. By far, however, most were drawn to the dynamic economic powerhouse and metropolis called Detroit, where the opportunity structure showed they were most needed. The historical similarities between Ukraine and southeastern Michigan were also appealing. Like Ukraine, southeastern Michigan generally (and Detroit specifically) owes its existence and early history to being a borderland among empires, in Detroit's case the British and French.

Michigan's borderland history goes back to 1701, the second year of the eighteenth century and seventy-five years before the United States declared its independence. "Detroit" means *strait* in French and refers to what is now the Detroit River, a narrow waterway linking Lake St. Clair and Lake Erie. Founded by Frenchman Antoine de la Mothe Cadillac, the city began as a fort named Fort Pontchartrain du détroit. On the urging of the French, Indigenous peoples gathered in the region. A fur trading center was established, which was coveted by the French, British, and, ultimately, American governments.[1] French fur trading, the extraction of natural resources, and the protection of this extraction by the French military were always the focus of Cadillac's endeavors and can be thought of as the first iteration of what would become a regionally complex opportunity structure. By 1707, Cadillac was actively appropriating lands, supervising claims for immigrant French settlers, and acting like a local baron by charging rent, requiring both fees and crop shares for the use of his mill, and providing competitive advantages for his own artisans.[2] By 1710 Cadillac's greed and corruption got him into trouble with the French government, and he was reposted to Louisiana, never to return. The city became a borderland of rivalries between not only the French and British, but also Indigenous nations, the most strident being the Fox and the Hurons. The French reinforced the fort and settlement but eventually, as their hold on North America weakened, lost control of the area to the British in 1760.[3] The area retained its strategic and commercial importance throughout the American revolutionary years, so much so that the British kept the settlement "in a sort of political limbo. Legally it was a United States possession, but the British continued to occupy it" until 1796, when "a detachment of American troops arrived . . . and the Stars and Stripes were hoisted," making Detroit "an American town at last."[4]

Destroyed by a fire in 1805, reorganized and rebuilt in the subsequent seven years, fought over in the war of 1812, and named a city in 1815, Detroit became "the funnel through which the settlers headed for the interior of Michigan . . . and during the 1820s and 1830s the reception of new arrivals was the city's most important business."[5] Michigan was given statehood and Detroit was established as the state capital in 1837.[6] In 1847, the state government decamped to Lansing when legislators complained about being impoverished by Detroit's cost of living.[7] Detroit retained its importance as a commercial center for surrounding agricultural land until the 1870s, when the opportunity structure began to diversify and manufacturing began to dominate, creating the growing and progressive opportunity structure requiring trainable and tractable workers, most of which would be recent immigrants from Central and Eastern Europe.

Thus, the Detroit that greeted Mykola Stefansky and other first-wave Ukrainian immigrants was already 184 years old and possessed a diverse culture with a complex economic base far advanced from its resource and agricultural beginnings. Still, as Olivier Zunz writes, "Detroit was . . . primarily a commercial center in the Great Lakes system of cities . . . with 116,340 inhabitants."[8] As noted, Stefansky was able to find an industrial job and within a few years to establish an independent tavern business for himself and his family. While it is not typical for a Ukrainian first-wave immigrant family to begin in mining and end up independently employed, Stefansky's experience is indicative of the career possibilities in a dynamic urban opportunity structure even as the network lines were establishing themselves. According to Zunz, Stefansky's success was because "Detroit in 1880 was still a multiethnic city in which class affiliations were secondary to people's ethnic attachments."[9] In other words, his and other Ukrainians' assimilation and progress depended first upon "networking" socially and economically with other Ukrainians.

Examining Detroit's situation in 1880 (ten years into the period of the first and largest wave of Ukrainian immigration to the United States), one can see that the region's eventual success waited only upon a vision of development and workers to enact it. Like other "major centers on the Great Lakes System . . . bounded on the east by the Pennsylvania coalfields and on the west by the iron ore reserves near Lake Superior"—Pittsburgh, Buffalo, Cleveland, and Milwaukee, in order of development (Detroit joined with Milwaukee in 1890)—Detroit was much favored by circumstances.[10] Zunz summarizes,

> Detroit was located near a wealth of natural resources in iron, copper, lead, and wood, most of which came from the upper part of the state, and near grindstone quarries and sand for glass. In part because of these nearby resources and in part because of the city's location as a port on the Great Lakes, Detroit had become a regional trading center by 1880. . . . [T]he Detroit River was an artery through which the commerce of lakes Superior, Michigan, and Huron was carried on toward Lake Erie and the Eastern Seaboard. In 1880, ten railroads connected Detroit to other parts of Michigan, to the rest of the country via Chicago, Milwaukee, Toledo, Cleveland, Buffalo, Indianapolis, and to the Canadian lines reaching New York and New England.[11]

In 1880, almost forty percent of Detroiters were foreign-born and consisted of forty different immigrant nationalities.[12] By 1881, Detroit was acquiring capacity in heavy industry as it began to lead the nation in stove manufacturing.[13] Also in 1881, Detroit had its first professional baseball team.[14] By 1884 electric arc street lighting brightened Jefferson and Woodward Avenues.[15] In 1889, Detroiters witnessed the completion of Detroit's first skyscraper, the ten-story Hammond building.[16] In the same year, Detroit could boast that it had a municipal power station serving the needs of streets, public buildings, and the electric streetcars that plied Woodward Avenue.[17] Three brief years later, in 1892, Detroit traffic traveled on asphalt on Jefferson, Lafayette, Cass, and Second streets.[18] In 1893, electricity was available for home lighting.[19]

On March 6, 1896, the first gas-powered automobile was driven on Detroit streets by Charles Brady King, while Henry Ford accomplished a similar feat three months later on June 4, 1896.[20] Beginning what would be a manufacturing and social revolution, changing Michigan and the lives of its growing Eastern European workforce forever, Ransom E. Olds established Detroit's first automobile factory. In 1903 his company would be joined by Ford, Cadillac, Buick, and Packard.[21] By this time, Detroit's opportunity structure and network lines provided career options for 285,704 people, making Detroit the thirteenth largest U.S. city. Nearly twelve percent of its citizens did not speak English and a significant number were, in fact, Poles, Russians, and Ukrainians, and many of these three national groups were Jews.[22] Detroit added to its world-leading stove manufacturing the diversified economy of "ship building, cigars and tobacco, pharmaceuticals, beer, rail cars, and foundry and machine shop products," which provided an increasingly large part of the opportunity structure offered to Ukrainian immigrants.[23] In 1925, only forty-five brief years since Stefansky's appearance and as the second-wave of Ukrainian immigrants had begun to arrive, "Detroit City . . . [was] home to three thousand major manufacturing plants, thirty-seven automobile manufacturing plants and two hundred and fifty auto accessory manufacturing plants."[24] The boom could not be accomplished without Eastern European immigration, among them first-wave Ukrainians:

> From 1900 to 1910 the primary source of population growth in Detroit and the surrounding region . . . [was] Eastern European immigration and white farmers moving into the city. During the 1910s automobile factories . . . [were] booming[,] resulting in Detroit more than doubling its population, [while] the region's population nearly double[d], surpassing one million people. By the end of the 1920s Detroit . . . [grew] in population . . . to over one and a half million people.[25]

The ethnic immigrant mix on the Ford Motor Company, January 12, 1917, sociological analysis roster provides some indication of the Ukrainian participation in the Detroit automobile "boom."[26] Of the fifty-eight different nationalities surveyed, "American" (presumably American-born citizens) ranks number one (16,457). "Ruthenians," very likely immigrants from the borderland of Western Ukraine (its border with Hungary), rank eighteenth in overall number, or 368 of the total 40,903 employees tabulated and analyzed. While Ruthenians are slightly less than one percent, groups including Ukrainians—Poles, Jews, Russians, Hungarians, and Austrians (Austro-Hungarians)—are more sizable. Respectively, they number 7525, 1437, 1160, 690, and 573. While it is impossible now to know exactly how many Ukrainians are among them, it would not be surprising if some of these immigrants were improperly identified and were from territories traditionally in the borderlands of southeastern Poland, southwestern Imperial Russia, and the eastern reaches of the Austro-Hungarian empire, which now would be considered Ukraine.[27] This is certainly true of those identified as Jews or Russian Jews. Jews in Ukraine typically spoke Russian, which was the dominant and official language of Imperial Russia and the territories it controlled. Robert Rockaway cites Russia as the primary source of Jewish immigration, with Romania second and Galicia, or Western Ukraine, third. Galicians were often "the poorest of the poor."[28] Their motivations were similar to anyone living in the Russian empire: "While many Jews fled home and country to escape violence, terror, and deprivation, others came to America because of its lure."[29] Taken together, Ruthenians, Poles, Jews, and Russians (the largest constituents of the Eastern European first-wave Slavs), as well as Austro-Hungarians, comprise 2.8 percent of the Ford Motor Company roster. While in 1917 the Ford Motor Company was already a large company, it was still only one of many. To say, then, that Eastern European immigrants played a significant part in Detroit's industrial economy is hardly overstatement. The rapid formation of mutual aid organizations is more evidence of Ukrainian participation in the workforce. The first fraternal lodge of the Ukrainian Workingmen's Association (#22) was formed on November 22, 1910. By 1916, on the eve of second-wave Ukrainian immigration, there were seven such lodges.[30] The Ukrainians' employment success is summarized by Stefaniuk and Dohrs:

> By the mid 1930's [the end of the second wave] some 25 to 30 thousand Ukrainians lived in the Detroit area . . . The majority of Detroit's Ukrainians were still employed in the auto industry—the assembly plants, machine shops, and steel factories in Hamtramck, Highland Park and north Detroit as well as in the Ford Rouge complex.[31]

Drawing upon Andrew M. Greeley's analysis of acculturation, Jaroslava Maria Petrykevich divides the assimilation of Detroit's first-wave Ukrainians into multiple phases.[32] The first phase is the survival or "cultural shock" phase, in which first-wave immigrants, exploited and disorientated, enter the workforce at its lowest levels, endure discrimination and ostracizing, live in what was typically the worst housing, and subsist on the most meager of resources.[33] The institutions that would eventually mitigate these conditions for first-wavers do not yet exist, for marginalized people are typically the last served. Depending upon the race of the immigrant, this first phase can be either brief or lengthy. In the case of Ukrainians, because they were neither people of color nor Asian (ethnic groups more actively oppressed, restricted, and segregated) and because of Detroit's rapidly expanding opportunity structures desperately needed them, this first phase for Ukrainians was passed through by Stefansky and his Ukrainian neighbors in approximately twenty years. As described by Petrykevich, the second phase is hallmarked by the appearance of mitigating and assimilating institutions par excellence, "church and mutual-aid societies":

> The Ukrainians attempted, as most ethnic groups in that time, to develop their own way of life around whatever institution that held the greatest promise of keeping their community together. The Church was therefore transformed into a central institution and what may be termed as the focal point of group activity in the new land. The church served as a community center around which a whole array of other institutional activities developed.[34]

The Church

Ukrainians, it turned out, were not easily assimilated into Latin Rite Roman Catholic churches, which were numerous because of Detroit's French and Polish immigrant heritage. Stefaniuk and Dohrs observe that

> Religion has always been a unique source of identity for Ukrainians. The nationalistic character, their distinct Ukrainian Rites[,] which included married priests and the use of the Ukrainian language in services, as well as a different calendar, set them apart from the adherents to the larger Latin Rite of the Roman Catholic church. Unable to understand and deal with these

differences, the local Roman Catholic hierarchy tended to reject Ukrainians . . . For this reason, unlike most other Slavic immigrants [Western and
Central European Slavs], Ukrainians resisted absorption into existing . . .
parishes. They longed for the solace . . . and familiarity of their own rite and
were motivated to build their own churches.[35]

Parish-building buttressed the growth of the two main Ukrainian neighborhoods. The first was Stefansky's, the oldest, in an area south of McGraw, west
of Livernois, and near Michigan Avenue. The second was on the east side near
the stronger, growing, and more contemporary opportunity structure north
of E. Grand Boulevard and south of Davison in the town of Hamtramck. Both
areas had also become the favorites of other Eastern European immigrants.

At first, Ukrainians clustered near available Roman Catholic parishes that
provided classes for English language learning, reading rooms with shared
books and periodicals, and venues for organizations and events. By 1905,
however, the small community begun by Mykola Stefansky was looking for
a place to satisfy its own specific religious needs.[36] A Jewish merchant from
Ukraine offered the basement of his synagogue for the Ukrainians' first services. In 1907, however, Stefansky "joined a committee to build a Ukrainian
Catholic Church for which he donated land on Cicotte Avenue."[37] His small
community built the first St. John's Ukrainian Catholic church on this land.
The first priest was Leo Levitsky. As the community drew immigrants from
the breadth of Ukraine, however, "a conflict developed between parishioners
as to the church's affiliation . . . and a group of dissidents left the parish."[38]
Stefaniuk and Dohrs explain that

> As the community grew from a small homogenous group of poor immi-
> grants primarily concerned with a satisfactory means of livelihood [in the
> first phase], into a larger, heterogenous social group, differences in personal
> preferences and ideologies became more pronounced [in the second phase].
> Clergy and laity alike, were often split along religious, nationalistic, and
> political lines. During this important period of growth, rivalries developed
> between Catholic and Orthodox Ukrainians causing divisions, and resulting
> in the building of new churches, sometimes within the same block.[39]

In 1911, orthodox-Christian Galicians from the Cicotte Avenue parish established a new parish on Gilbert and Clayton streets. This parish identified with

First Russian Orthodox Church, circa 1908. Gilbert and Clayton Streets, Ss. Peter and Paul Church. (COURTESY OF FR. PAUL ALBERT AT PRESENT-DAY SS. PETER AND PAUL ORTHODOX CATHEDRAL. USED WITH PERMISSION.)

First St. John the Baptist Ukrainian Catholic Church in Detroit, Michigan, 3564 Cicotte Ave. Circa 1907. (COURTESY OF UKRAINIAN AMERICAN ARCHIVES AND MUSEUM. USED WITH PERMISSION.)

Russian orthodoxy.[40] The original St. John's Ukrainian Catholic parish on Cicotte became too small, so parishioners built a new St. John's church on Clippert and Edward streets.

Ukrainian ethnic cohesiveness, however, was always stressed by economic necessity. Zunz describes how "the native white Americans [who controlled industry] undermined the possibilities of mobility *within* a group for a large section of Detroit's work force [my emphasis]."[41] These established industrialists built new plants in other neighborhoods, causing the ethnic communities to expand, split, and move, challenging an ethnic group's ability to remain cohesive.[42] At first parishes ameliorated the disruption, drawing people back together. For example, the movement of jobs to Detroit's east side, and the consequent movement of people to the Hamtramck and Highland Park areas, led to the establishment of a new parish, the first Immaculate Conception Ukrainian Catholic Church on Hamtramck's Grayling Avenue. It celebrated its first mass on Palm Sunday in 1914.[43] As the population grew and spread, so did the churches that served them. Ukrainian-associated parishes and churches include the following.[44]

Present-day St. John the Baptist Ukrainian Catholic Church, Clippert and Edward.

Ukrainian Catholic Churches

St. John the Baptist

St. John the Baptist Ukrainian Catholic Church began as a parcel of land gifted to Mykola Stefansky at 3564 Cicotte Avenue in Stefansky's neighborhood on Detroit's west side. Stefansky, in turn, donated it for Detroit's first Ukrainian Catholic parish. He and his sons built the frame church, which opened in the spring of 1908. By 1918 church growth dictated an additional parish, and a new church on Clippert and Edward was built. It was consecrated in 1920, drawing its membership from both the Cicotte Avenue parish and second-wave arrivals to the Detroit area. In 1933 the Cicotte Avenue church was auctioned off, and in the same year the Clippert and Edward parish added a school. Facing declining enrollments and financial concerns, the school closed in 1986.

Immaculate Conception

Immaculate Conception Ukrainian Catholic Church is on Detroit's east side and was built to serve the increasing Ukrainian American populations in the Hamtramck area. The first parish house was a small, frame church on Grayling Street. It celebrated its first liturgy on April 12, 1914. A school and community center, the Krasinski Khatam, next to the church was completed on July 15, 1917. Growth in the parish in the ensuing decades meant expansion, so building lots and an estate were purchased for a convent and high school, which opened in 1959. Construction and decoration were completed in 1976 and the church was consecrated on May 23 of that year. Because of population shifts to the northern suburbs in the 1980s, a parish grade school was purchased in Warren, and the former grade school in Hamtramck was converted to a high school.

St. Josaphat

St. Josaphat Ukrainian Catholic Church in Warren came into being because of the population shifts already referred to. In 1958, services were held in rented school facilities and the St. Cletus Roman Catholic Church. Parishioners built a church in 1964 and a rectory in 1976. In the 1980s, parishioners refurbished the church. Since 1987 the parish has cooperated with the

Immaculate Conception Ukrainian Catholic Church, Hamtramck. (COURTESY OF PAUL M.
HEDEEN. © PAUL M. HEDEEN. USED WITH PERMISSION.)

Immaculate Conception parish in sponsoring the Sunflower Festival held on
the St. Josaphat property each year.

St. Michael the Archangel

Population shifts west from the St. John neighborhood to the Dearborn
area prompted Ukrainian Catholics to create St. Michael the Archangel
parish. From 1952 until 1964, services were held in facilities on Horger and
Clay roads.[45] In 1964, however, the parishioners celebrated their Christmas
masses in their new church. The church was remodeled in a more Byzantine
style and was consecrated again on November 19, 1983.

Our Lady of Perpetual Help Ukrainian Catholic Church

The continued spread of Ukrainian parishioners into Detroit's western
suburbs prompted St. John the Baptist Church to create Our Lady of Perpetual Help, a missionary church in Dearborn Heights. Future parishioners
purchased land in January 1962, and the new building was consecrated on
April 21, 1963, as a mission church. In October 1967, the church became

St. Mary Protectress Ukrainian Orthodox Cathedral, Southfield, Michigan. (COURTESY OF UKRAINIAN AMERICAN ARCHIVES AND MUSEUM. USED WITH PERMISSION.)

independent, and English-only services were offered, while Ukrainian language classes were revived.

Ukrainian Orthodox Churches

St. Mary Protectress Ukrainian Orthodox Cathedral

The organizational meeting for a Ukrainian Orthodox parish was held on March 17, 1950, by third-wave Ukrainians. In 1951 the parish acquired its own facility on 29th Street near Michigan Avenue, on the north end of the original west-side Ukrainian neighborhood. There were immediate plans for expansion into a proposed new building. The new St. Mary Protectress Cathedral was completed and consecrated in 1970 at 21931 Evergreen Road in Southfield.

Holy Trinity Ukrainian Orthodox Church

This west-side parish was organized in September 1939. In December 1943, a city block of land was purchased at Michigan and Ogden for permanent

St. Andrew's Ukrainian Orthodox Church. (COURTESY OF MARYNA HEDEEN. © MARYNA HEDEEN. USED WITH PERMISSION.)

buildings, but the building restrictions caused by World War II delayed construction. The parish purchased buildings on Humboldt Avenue and sold its land. This facility was sold in 1952, and the parish relocated to Dearborn's Normile Avenue. The cornerstone was laid on July 25, 1954, with the first liturgy celebrated on October 30 of that same year. In 1959 the parish completed the rectory. Due to declining numbers of attendees, the parish was forced to close its doors in the summer of 2014.[46]

St. Andrew Ukrainian Orthodox Church

Eighty-two third-wave immigrants opened St. Andrew's Ukrainian Orthodox Church in a rented facility in Hamtramck on November 10, 1951, and the church was officially registered on January 14 of the following year. A new church was built at 5130 Prescott Street and celebrated its first service on December 7, 1958. The parish was consecrated on May 31, 1959, and has been associated with the Ukrainian Bandurist Chorus of Detroit and the Women's Bandurist Ensemble. The parish's children have also supported and attended the Ridna Shkola Ukrainian heritage school.

Protestant Churches

Two Protestant churches were important to Ukrainians of the second-wave and third-wave immigrations. The First Ukrainian Baptist Church in Detroit was in operation in 1923. The Ukrainian Evangelical Reformed Church of Detroit served Ukrainians in the 1950s, but neither is in operation today.

Mutual Aid

In 1914 Ukrainian east-siders began constructing a school and social hall on Grayling Avenue. The Ukrainian Home was dedicated in July of 1917 and provided the first location for Immaculate Conception Church and the site for a growing list of enlightenment programs concerning art, literature, drama, and choral music. The Home's reading room became a place to gather, peruse recent newspapers and periodicals, and discuss politics and current American and Ukrainian events.[47]

The formation of mutual aid or fraternal societies is an impulse that can be traced back to earlier first-wave Ukrainians in New York and Pennsylvania.[48]

Like Ukraine itself, the organizations divided themselves into independent and pro-Russian organizations, at least ten of the former and five of the latter.[49] All had significant assets and served Ukrainian workingmen and women by paying out death or disability benefits, looking after Ukrainian families, and supporting social and political causes associated with first- and second-wave Ukrainian immigrants. Mutual Aid societies active in Detroit include The Ukrainian Workingmen's Association (1913, the name was changed to Ukrainian Fraternal Association), Ukrainian National Aid Association (1920), Ukrainian Providence Association (1920), and Ukrainian National Association (1907).[50]

Mutual Aid societies and service groups are linked to several Detroit landmarks. The Ukrainian American Center began in the basement of a Hamtramck church. In 1917, as described above, it moved to the Ukrainian Home on Grayling Avenue. The Ukrainian Home Association was replaced in name and location in 1928 when the organization secured property at 2965 Carpenter Street. In 1931 the cornerstone for the Ukrainian Worker's Home was laid. Later the name was changed back to the Ukrainian American Center. Meeting rooms, a bar, and a concert venue hosted hundreds of events until the building was sold in 1985.

Ukrainian National Association members combined their efforts to build, furnish, equip, and utilize the Ukrainian National Temple located at 4655 Martin Street. The Temple was dedicated on January 16, 1938, when Detroit's Ukrainian neighborhoods were at their height of unity and prosperity and the second wave, the political émigrés in Ukrainian immigration, had joined and begun contributing to Detroit's Ukrainian community. This facility was a four-year project of four local Ukrainian National Association of America branches and many local Ukrainian-owned businesses in Southwest Detroit. The Temple was used during the World War II years for Red Cross and Torch drives, wartime bond sales, and, following the war, as a destination for many third-wave Ukrainian immigrants as they arrived to begin their new lives as refugees fleeing Europe and Soviet Ukraine. The building hosted scores of public and private events on Detroit's west side and was sold and repurposed as a nightclub and now a Pentecostal church.[51]

The parishes, along with mutual aid societies and brick-and-mortar community halls, helped Ukrainians resist for a time what Zunz considered inevitable: "a major restructuring of social relationships" in ethnic groups

Icons

Icons are depictions of Jesus, Mary, the apostles, or the saints. Pictured as well are symbolic histories and life lessons. Icons are considered sacred and often are blessed at the church.* They differ according to their purpose: some are made for households, while others are created for decoration and liturgical use at the church or monastery, and they are purchased or given as gifts to commemorate the most important events in a parishioner's life. Icons protect the owner from evil spirits and bring blessings, wealth, and health. Most Ukrainian households worldwide have at least one icon, regardless of how religious the household is. The icons often are valued more as a traditional object of veneration than as a mystical charm, much like every Protestant home will have a family Bible even if it is seldom read.

The tradition of icon "writing" is very old and dates to the fourth century. Ukrainian icons, like other ethnic icons, have unique features that vary according to the region and era of their creation. Therefore, many schools and styles of Ukrainian icons have emerged. Some of them were produced by artists associated directly with the church and some were created by folk artists. Church or canonical icons are influenced directly by the preferences of the clergy for a particular saint or style of depiction. Icons created by folk artists might use national colors, floral and other regional designs, and regional depictions of the saints' clothing, poses, and facial features. In general, Ukrainian folk icons are known for their kind representations of simple people.†

Icons are collectible and will often be treasured as a centerpiece in the homes of Michigan's Ukrainians. Older and rarer examples are still collected and valued by wealthy Ukrainians all over the world. In fact, Ukrainian immigrants everywhere have been instrumental in preserving Ukrainian icons during Soviet times and developing new icon writing styles since the 1930s. Not only did Michigan's Ukrainians bring their icons when they emigrated to the United States, but they also brought back additional ones with each visit to the old country, especially during Soviet times. While Ukrainian church doors were closed from the 1930s to the 1980s, Michigan's Ukrainian Americans were building new churches with icons as their centerpieces.‡ Michiganders have joined the larger Ukrainian diaspora in helping to finance the preservation and restoration of old icons in Ukraine and worldwide.

Ukrainian icons in Michigan were painted by renowned local artists Mykhailo Dmytrenko, George and Jerome Kozak, and various artists from New

York.[§] Recently, the interest in icons has been revived, and those created by famous artists have become popular in both churches and private homes and can easily be purchased online from artists or church gift shops.

* Maureen Mostyn Liebenson, *Christmas in Ukraine* (Chicago: World Book, Inc., 1997), 29.
† "Mother of God in Icons and Old Prints," The National Center of Folk Culture "Ivan Honchar Museum," https://honchar.org.ua/events/bohorodytsya-v-narodnij-ikoni-ta-starodrukah.
‡ Bohdan Tymkiv and Roksolana Tymkiv, "Sacral Wood Carving of Ukrainian Artists of the Western Diaspora." *Scientific Notes of Ostroh Academy*, ser. Historical Sciences (2015). https://journals.oa.edu.ua/Historical/article/view/1427.
§ Ksenia Rychtycka, "Michigan History Conference Spotlights Local Ukrainian Community," *Ukrainian Weekly*, March 24, 2017. George and Jerome Kozak are the celebrated artist sons of Edward Kozak, who is described in chapter 5 of this book.

"as new divisions based on social class grew more important."[52] Religious differences notwithstanding, Ukrainians and their parishes, parish schools, and all associated mutual aid organizations helped first- and then second-wave Ukrainian immigrants remain "free from the threat of organized class conflicts despite extreme inequality of conditions."[53] This institutional and ethnic solidarity weakened the need and impact of labor unions, at least until the Depression in 1929 forced massive layoffs and created dire economic situations midway through the Ukrainian immigrants' second wave. During the Depression, the parishes and mutual aid societies helped sustain Ukrainian Michiganders until social programming and late-1930s, World War II rearmament created an economic resurgence in Detroit and throughout the Midwest.

As in the old country (and in many orthodox cultures), gender roles, especially for first- and second-wave immigrants, tended to be rigid. Most Ukrainian men worked in local industry and commerce, for southeastern Michigan's opportunity structure grew significantly as the automobile industry transformed and then dominated Detroit's onetime diversified manufacturing. In 1900, approximately when the automobile assembly industry began, only 3.8 percent of the total number of Detroit's factory workers built cars.[54] This number increased "eightfold" by 1909, and in five more years, at the close of Ukrainian immigration's first wave, the 3.8 percent had reached 40 percent.[55] In fact, "Auto manufacturing," according to Rockaway, "transformed Detroit from a diversified trade and manufacturing city into a one-industry town."[56] For the majority of women not working in manufacturing, the experience was different.

Michigan's Ukrainian Immigrants and Religion

Ukraine's Christian traditions began over a thousand years ago with the Christianization of the Kyivan Rus (Ukraine's medieval state).* Over many centuries, Christianity was gradually superimposed over a complex body of pagan oral and written literatures that included minstrel tales, pantheistic folklore, and courtly legends. Latent pagan narratives and seasonal practices helped people subsume Christian ethical and moral precepts and bring them into Ukraine's already rich symbolic culture.† In Ukraine, worshippers might adhere to the teachings, liturgy, and ceremonial practices of no less than four separate orthodox denominations; also existent are Islam, Judaism, and a number of Protestant sects like Baptists, Quakers, and Mormons.

Michigan's Ukrainian parishioners might practice any of the above faiths. Distinctly Ukrainian parishes, however, reflect the competing orthodoxies of the old country and their histories. The earliest church was begun and spread by the apostles proselytizing in very different cultures, first in Judaic Jerusalem and pagan Rome, then in Antioch, Roman Syria, and, through the travels of the Apostle Paul, in what is now called Turkey and Greece, gathering indigenous influences along the way.‡ Two primary traditions evolved: the Western or "Latin" and the Eastern or "Greek."§ When in 325 AD Roman Emperor Constantine moved the imperial capital and church from Rome to Constantinople (Istanbul), he spread Rome's ecclesiastical authority to the East and drew to it Eastern traditions and influences. This created a division in the Eastern churches, one "Byzantine" group looking toward Rome, the other toward Antioch, Alexandria, and Jerusalem.

Four "orthodox" traditions remain in Michigan's Ukrainian community today: Roman Catholic (Western and Latin); Ukrainian Catholic (Byzantine or Greek), recognizing Rome's authority; Ukrainian Orthodox, recognizing a Constantinople patriarch; and Russian Orthodox, recognizing a Moscow patriarch. Michigan's Ukrainian Orthodox Christians may choose to worship in any of the four. The Roman Catholics, influenced by Latin Rite Catholicism from Poland, worship in any Roman Catholic church. They follow the Gregorian calendar and the Latin rite. Services are now mostly in English (only a few Latin services are offered). Priests are not allowed to marry. Ukrainian Catholics recognize Rome's papal authority but follow a Byzantine rite and the Julian calendar. The

Ukrainian language is used, although sparingly. In contrast to Roman Catholic priests, Ukrainian Catholic priests can marry.

"Orthodox" Ukrainians may worship in either Ukrainian or Russian orthodox churches, with the latter having grown in Ukraine via the oppressive influence of Imperial Russia.[¶] Ukrainian Orthodox and Russian Orthodox churches follow a Byzantine rite and Julian calendar, and recognize the authority of a patriarchy. As already noted, the Ukrainian Orthodox church follows the Ecumenical Patriarch of Constantinople. The Russian Orthodox church follows the Patriarch of Moscow. Ukrainian Orthodox churches use Slavonic and Ukrainian languages, while Russian orthodox churches use Slavonic and Russian languages. As with Ukrainian Catholicism, Ukrainian and Russian Orthodox priests can marry.

* George Gajecky, "One Thousand Years of Christianity in Ukraine," *Ukrainians in Detroit and Michigan: Commemorating the Millennium of Christianity in Ukraine* (Detroit: Metropolitan Detroit Ukrainian Millennium Council, 1988), 6.
† Ibid.
‡ "About Byzantine Catholics," St. Michael Ukrainian Catholic Church, https://stmichaelgrandrapids.org/about.
§ Ibid.
¶ Jim Nakonechny, Rev., "Ask a Priest," Ukrainian Catholic Eparchy of Edmonton, September 8, 2020.

Reassured by the presence of mutual aid societies, Michigan's Ukrainian women built and sustained a culture that was, at first, centered upon home, parish, and (where available) school. This culture intentionally fostered appreciation and enthusiasm for both Ukrainian values and the gradual assimilation of Ukrainian children into American life. Immigrant preoccupations moved into what Greeley and Petrykevich called a third phase. Individuals and then groups became conscious of the opportunity to attain higher economic and cultural status, most often moving from working class to middle class.[57] Petrykevich describes how in the third phase "the more talented and gifted individuals . . . [began] to break out of the ethnic group and find their way into the mainstream of American society. During this stage the Ukrainian immigrants were most interested in the formation of social organizations."[58]

Leading the way in this formation were immigrant women, who provided leadership for the ethnic group, forming their own organizations and creating "the matrix for the development . . . of most of the organizations and projects of the Ukrainian American community."[59] Women's groups tended to be both dynamic and enlightenment-focused and, absorbing the politics of the second wave, involved in "tireless fund raising efforts . . . for many Ukrainian causes here in the United States and Ukraine."[60] Among the women's organizations was the Prosvita Women's Educational Society, "organized in 1921 to promote education and enlightenment among Ukrainian women. They held weekly meetings where lectures on a variety of cultural topics were presented, sponsored Ukrainian and English language classes and aided many causes with funds and work."[61] Another popular women's group was the Ukrainian National Women's League of America (organized in 1929, during the Ukrainian second wave), which, at its peak, had eleven chapters in the metropolitan area of Detroit and two auxiliary chapters in outlying cities.[62] These chapters not only donated money and time to Ukrainian institutions but also represented "the Ukrainian-American community . . . [in] American society by organizing cultural and Ukrainian folk art exhibitions, teaching Ukrainian crafts and folk dancing[,] and working with American women's organizations."[63]

Ukrainian groups including both men and women grew with the population. Some helped organizations facilitating Ukrainian immigrants' efforts at naturalization, among them "the Ukrainian Citizens' League, The American Citizens' Club[,] the Ukrainian Citizens' Youth Club[,] and many others."[64] The climax of this activism was the establishment in 1939 of the Federation of Ukrainian Organizations of the State of Michigan, which had "the mandate to coordinate the activities of and represent the three groupings of Ukrainian organizations in the Detroit area."[65] These groupings, which taken together were the *realpolitik* of the Ukrainian diaspora, included (1) the Ukrainian Social Council, "which represented the more progressive democratic organizations" of Detroit's Ukrainian Americans; (2) "the Central Committee of Ukrainian National Organizations . . . which included all of the branches of the Organization for the Rebirth of Ukraine and all the area branches of the Ukrainian National Association"; and (3) the "conservative, nationalistic . . . Ukrainian American Political Club . . . Ukrainian Providence Association, most church organizations[,] and the Ukrainian Hetman Association of America."[66] On the verge of World War II and its decade-long curtailing of Ukrainian immigration (the third wave would begin in 1948), the Federation marked the high point of political and social organization for Detroit's first- and second-wave Ukrainians.[67] The Federation accomplished its goal of consolidating the Ukrainian community and providing "for more efficient use of resources for the different projects and for more effective representation of the Ukrainian community in the multicultural mosaic of Metropolitan Detroit."[68] The Federation's organizations,

> including the religious ones, regardless of their specific agenda and goals, emphasized the same basic ideals, namely to enable their members to become more useful and productive American citizens while maintaining their Ukrainian identity, to help their native land in all ways possible, to protest the injustices being committed by foreign governments in Ukraine[,] and to inform and educate the American public about Ukraine.[69]

The Federation financially supported schools and educational organizations in Ukraine; the Sheptytsky Hospital in Lviv; and "war veterans, invalids, widows[,] and orphans"; and it facilitated bond and blood drives during World War II.[70] The Federation helped to center Detroit's Ukrainians in the city's community life. It "sponsored civic activities, promoted charitable and cultural events, and assisted in fund-raising campaigns to promote the well-being of not only the Ukrainian community but the city at large."[71] The Federation participated in the "50th anniversary of the founding of the automobile industry, International Nights, Detroit News Travel Shows," and events directly focused upon Ukrainian assimilation, such as "I Am An American Day."[72] During the war, Michigan's Ukrainian Women's organizations so fully supported Red Cross blood drives and fundraising that these organizations earned "the honor of displaying the Ukrainian flag along side [sic] the other nationality flags at the main headquarters of the American Red Cross."[73] In Michigan's postwar era, the Federation devoted significant volunteer time to "different Ukrainian candidates in their bid for . . . state representative seats and judgeships."[74]

In addition to the parish-building, joining mutual-aid associations, acquiring facilities, and filling the rosters of the women's organizations just described, Ukrainians, both men and women, supported other important Ukrainian-American Federation organizations closely associated with first- and second-wave immigrants:[75]

- Social clubs: Pontiac (1941), Ukrainian Women's League of America (1938), Ukrainian Women's Educational Society (1921), Ukrainian Michigan League (1938), Ukrainian American Social Club (1936), Ukrainian Club Orlyk (1937), Veterans Association (1931).

- Cultural organizations: Ukrainian Graduates (1939), Wayne State University Ukrainian Club (1938).
- Political organizations: Ukrainian Democratic Club of Wayne County (1932).

First- and second-wave groups deserving more detailed mention are described next.

The Ukrainian Club at Wayne State University

The Ukrainian Club at Wayne State University (WSU) was organized in 1938 by then student Michael Wichorek. It soon grew from twenty-three members to seventy-five and became the oldest club of Ukrainian college students in the United States.[76] Its primary purposes were to unite students of Ukrainian descent, promote events of interest to Ukrainian American students, and serve as a promoter of and liaison to Ukrainian community groups. For many years, "Ukrainian Night"—an introduction of university students to Ukrainian heritage, culture, and struggle for political freedom—was its central event.

Now called the "Wayne State University Slavic Klub," the organization "is for WSU students interested in all things Slavic. Members have the opportunity to learn more about different Slavic cultures (such as Russian, Ukrainian, Slovak, Bosnian, Macedonian, Serbian, Croatian, and Polish)."[77]

The Ukrainian Graduates

Graduates of WSU of Ukrainian heritage established the Ukrainian Graduates organization in October of 1939.[78] Its purpose over the years has been to continue the good work of the Ukrainian club as a liaison and promoter of Ukrainian cultural events and to support WSU students with loans, grants, and scholarships. The scholarship fund, begun in 1941, combines the club's purposes of promoting both Ukrainian culture and higher education. It has awarded more than 500 scholarships. The organization has also "initiated and supported drives to aid Ukrainian studies at various institutions."[79] Since 1955 the organization has annually recognized an outstanding citizen of the Ukrainian community at large. The organization's The Graduate Bulletin was begun in 1940 by Martha Wichorek and has had many editors. It has continued since 2000 under the editorship of Ms. Olga Meyer.

The Ukrainian Room at Wayne State University

WSU sponsors a number of ethnic heritage rooms. Among them is the Ukrainian Room, which was established and dedicated on September 24, 1976.[80] It showcases Ukrainian art and culture. The Ukrainian Graduates of Detroit · and Windsor refurbished the room in 1999 and rededicated it in 2003. It still exists but is no longer sponsored or funded due to decreased academic interest in the Ukrainian language.[81]

Institutions and the Third Wave

The Federation of Ukrainian Organizations supported the work of the Ukrainian Congress Committee of America (UCCA), "the first relief agency for resettling Ukrainian [third-wave] displaced persons."[82] The UCCA was a national group, according to Petrykevich, "sponsored by four leading [Ukrainian] fraternal organizations . . . the Ukrainian National Association of Jersey City, New Jersey; the Ukrainian National Aid Association of Pittsburgh, Pennsylvania; the Providence Association of Ukrainian Catholics of Pennsylvania; and the Ukrainian Workingmen's Association of Scranton, Pennsylvania."[83] In addition to facilitating the third wave of Ukrainian immigration after World War II, the UCCA wholeheartedly supported the United States' foreign policy and military strategy during the war and pledged itself to defeating European totalitarianism while advancing, as always, the cause of Ukrainian independence. The UCCA also sponsored and supported American political candidates most likely to be sympathetic to the wishes of the Ukrainian diaspora.[84] Partnered with the Federation, Michiganders in the UCCA became the perfect network line for third-wave Ukrainian refugees languishing in Europe during the late 1940s.

Upon arrival, third-wave refugees faced sudden and pressing challenges. These men and women (and children) had not been able to plan, gather funds, or sell belongings in Ukraine. In most cases, they could rely on no family member to shepherd and shelter them. Physically, socially, and historically they had been displaced, afraid to go home to a devastated Ukraine, a "bloodland" now being rapidly and completely repressed, Russified, and Sovietized.[85] They must have wondered where they would work and live, especially how they would rekindle careers commensurate with their professional education and training.[86] Moreover, true assimilation required more than textbook knowledge of American language and culture, but a vernacular fluency in both. Impoverished, they also lacked the luxury of time.[87] They had to work and take what jobs they could.

Third-wavers were also not helped by the widespread American ignorance of Europe and its hundreds of ethnic groups, the histories of countries Americans struggled even to locate on a map, and the terrible distrust, even hatred, of peoples and cultures closely associated with recent enemies of the United States. After all, Romania, Hungary, and Austria, which had controlled parts of Ukraine, once served alongside Nazi Germany. Significant numbers of nationalistic Ukrainians had served in the German Army as *Osttruppen* and in local defense battalions and police forces, and some had even been *Trawniki* men. It should be noted that some defense battalions, police forces, and *Trawniki* squads were active collaborators in the repression and murder of Jews.[88] And there was in some cases an association of third-wavers with the Warsaw Pact nations, NATO's new enemies (since 1949), including Western, Central, and Eastern Slavs who were being ideologized by a repressive and vengeful USSR. It didn't help that most religious third-wavers attended orthodox churches, which were looked upon with suspicion by a reawakened midcentury American nativism.

Third-wave Ukrainians, however, were smart, resourceful survivors. Petrykevich notes that

> The "New" Ukrainian immigrants almost immediately upon arrival began forming organizations of a variety of categories. For example, between 1948 and 1950 the "New" immigrants formed a total of eight organizations—of which one was a mutual aid organization, three were political organizations, two were work-oriented organizations[,] and two were cultural-secular organizations.[89]

This activism can be attributed to the immigrants' immediate needs. Isolated and fearing being trapped in jobs associated with much lower educational and professional statuses, the immigrants needed to network, recertify, and sustain themselves, at least near the professional level they had enjoyed in the old country. Having endured the antihuman ideologies and governments of Central and Eastern Europe and witnessed the drawbacks of passivity, the new immigrants took an immediate interest in U.S. and Ukrainian politics. These immigrants' intellectuality and cultural sophistication also needed expression. They were familiar and comfortable with the organizational life of advanced urban cultures. Moreover, they wanted to reawaken for their children the very organizations that had served them so well back home.[90]

While they also welcomed members from earlier immigrant groups, three Michigan parishes were established with the arrival of third-wavers: Our Lady of Perpetual Help Ukrainian Catholic Church (1962), St. Michael's Ukrainian Catholic Church (1951), and St. Andrew's Ukrainian Orthodox Church (1952). Joining these supportive parishes, the Self-reliance Credit Union Association (1949) was established to provide independent financial aid.

From the late 1940s through the 1960s, organizations of all kinds were formed. Reflecting the tumult and paradoxes of the post-World War II world, they were vibrantly progressive *and* nostalgic, yet distinctly different than groups focused on economic opportunity (first-wave) or political freedom (second-wave). A partial list follows.[91]

- Professional groups: the Ukrainian Teachers Association (1965), Ukrainian Engineers Association (1948), Ukrainian Medical Association (1950), and the Ukrainian Pharmacists Association (1969).
- Political organizations: Plast (1949), SUMA (1950), and the Union of Former Members of the Ukrainian Insurgent Army (1954).
- Cultural organizations: Ukrainian Educational Society (1950), Ukrainian Studies Chair Fund (1965), Ukrainian Music Institute (1954), Ukrainian Bandurist Chorus (1949), Ukrainian Trembita Chorus (1957), Ukrainian Academy of Arts and Sciences (1960), and the Ukrainian Folk Dance Ensemble (1948).

Other third-wave groups deserving more detailed mention are described in the following sections.

The Ukrainian Cultural Center (Formerly the Ukrainian Home)

Located at 26601 Ryan Road, Warren, Michigan, the Ukrainian Cultural Center (UCC) consists of a conference and dining venue, "the heart of the Ukrainian community in the Southeastern Michigan area—a meeting

Ukrainian Home, 2240 Grayling Street, Immaculate Conception Founders blessing, July 15, 1917. Ukrainian Home housed classes and clergy of Immaculate Conception Ukrainian Catholic Church. (COURTESY OF UKRAINIAN AMERICAN ARCHIVES AND MUSEUM. USED WITH PERMISSION.)

place for members of the community and the community's organizations, and the central information point for activities within the local area."[92] The UCC opens its doors to anyone wishing to rent its space and "to individuals and organizations of all cultures and creeds for music and dance activities, lecture and exhibit activities, weddings, showers, and a gathering point for community members."[93] In doing so, the UCC prides itself in highlighting and promoting Ukrainian Americans and their accomplishments through time. The Ryan Road UCC is the most recent iteration of centers previously located on Grayling and Carpenter streets. The Ryan Road building was re-modeled in 1978 and 2004.[94]

The Ukrainian American Archives and Museum

The UAAM was established in 1958 in a former bank building on Woodward Avenue.[95] The facility was relocated to the corner of Commor and Charest Street near Immaculate Conception Church. The structure was acquired by

Embroidery

Embroidery is the most famous and common form of folk art in Ukraine and in Ukrainian communities worldwide, including those in Michigan. Ukrainian embroidery is well recognized and has inspired multiple international fashion couture collections (e.g., Gucci, Dior, Sportmax, and Valentino, to name a few).[*] Unlike European Ukraine, which was forced to suppress folk arts during Soviet times, immigrant communities have always maintained an interest in embroidery. In Ukraine and throughout the world, artists embroider costumes, ritual cloths (rushnyky, pronounced ruh-sh-NYHK), and other items, since embroidered goods have become a sign of ethnic identification both in Ukraine and around the world. Typically, citizens of the Ukrainian diaspora can afford to pay for these handmade goods. They are also among the most generous buyers of antiques, paying two hundred to two thousand dollars for embroidered shirts and gowns made in the nineteenth and early twentieth centuries. Collectors of Ukrainian embroidery from Michigan include Dr. Miroslaw and Anna Hantiuk, who have been traveling to Ukraine since the 1980s and have acquired a large collection of folk-art objects including embroidered gowns and rushnyky. They recently donated their collection to the Ukrainian American Archives and Museum in Hamtramck, Michigan, and to the Ukrainian Museum Archives in Cleveland, Ohio.[†]

Ukrainian embroidery dates to pre-Christian times, when Slavs believed that embroidered ornaments in clothing and various household textiles (e.g., pillowcases, napkins, and tablecloths) would protect them from evil spirits and bring blessings to their owners. Thus, designs, patterns, color combinations, and even stitches have pre-Christian meanings. In Christian times, embroidery has taken on both secular and sacred uses.[‡] Embroidery is the main characteristic of rushnyky that are "used in folk customs and rites . . . particularly for weddings and for decorating holy icons. Embroidered kerchiefs were used in funerals for covering the face of the deceased."[§] Church embroidery includes rushnyky (for draping icons and crosses), chasubles, stoles, and veils. Distinct techniques, colors, and patterns vary greatly by region and have been evolving with time.[¶] In general, cheaper materials were used by the poor, while the rich and the church could even afford gold and silver threads along with very expensive fabrics. Embroidery is mainly done by women. While it was preferable for every woman to know how to embroider, the most talented artists ran small businesses since there were always customers for high-quality embroidery.

* Liana Satenstein, "Ukraine's Influence on the Runway Is Bigger Than You Think," *Vogue*, February 1, 2017.
† "Hantiuk Collection," Ukrainian American Archives and Museum, https://www.ukrainianmuseumdetroit.org/copy-of-hnatiuk-collection.
‡ Demian Horniatkevych and Lidiia Nenadkevych, "Embroidery," *Encyclopedia of Ukraine*, vol. 1 (Toronto: University of Toronto Press, 1984).
§ Ibid.
¶ "Ukrainian Embroidery," Textile Research Center, https://www.trc-leiden.nl/trc-needles/regional-traditions/europe-and-north-america/embroideries/ukrainian-embroidery.

third-wave immigrant Roman Dacko and his wife, who began building the collection. A branch of the museum once was located at the UCC on Ryan Road but was reconsolidated at the Commor/Charest Street location. Now the museum is located at 9630 Joseph Campau Street in Hamtramck.

The museum has an extensive collection of Ukrainian ceramics, embroidery, documents, and photographs representing the life of Ukrainian diaspora immigrants in the Detroit area. It also serves as an archive comprising of an extensive collection of 20,000 books on "the Ukrainian immigration to the United States and the contributions of Americans of Ukrainian descent to America." The museum is an active cultural center featuring exhibits, literary readings, and tours. The exhibits focus on folk art (embroidery, pysanky, ceramics), important events in the history of Ukraine (Chornobyl nuclear accident, the Holodomor, and the Russian Federation's invasions of Crimea and Eastern Ukraine), and works of Ukrainian artists.[96]

Dibrova (The Oak Grove)

For sixty years Ukrainian Americans have owned and utilized this retreat location near Brighton, Michigan. A small lifetime fee is charged for access to anyone with a Ukrainian connection. Part of the land is privately developed. The other part, according to Myrosia Stefaniuk, includes the Zelenyj Yar (the Green Valley, the Plast or scout camp), "a pavilion and kitchen, an athletic field, volleyball court, playground, rental units, a beach, and an old dock by the lake."[97]

Plast

Founded in 1949 as a third-wave expression of Ukrainian culture and values, Plast is the Ukrainian version of the Boy and Girl Scouts. Plast follows
the legacy of the organization founded in 1911 in Ukraine by Dr. Oleksandr
Tysovskyj.[98] Because the organization requires knowledge of Ukrainian language, history, and culture, it is affiliated with Ukrainian schools. Otherwise,
Plast resembles the Boy and Girls Scouts in its values, activities, uniforms,
and reward structures.[99] Plast supports the following three fundamental
principles: "To be faithful to God and Ukraine," "To help others," and "To
live by the Plast Code and obey Plast leadership."[100] Plast teaches fourteen
character traits:

1. Keeping one's word
2. Conscientiousness
3. Accuracy
4. Frugality
5. Fairness
6. Politeness
7. Brotherliness and well-wishing
8. Equanimity
9. Usefulness
10. Obedience to Plast leadership
11. Attentiveness
12. Caring for one's health
13. Loving and caring for beauty
14. Positive thinking at all times.[101]

Like the Boy and Girl Scouts, Plast divides itself according to gender and age.
Outdoor Plast activities are often held at Dibrova.

Ukrainian Bandurist Chorus

The Ukrainian Bandurist Chorus had its origins in Ukraine in the early twentieth century, first in Kharkiv in 1902, then Kyiv in 1918, and thirdly in Poltava
in 1923. Because the group chose to participate in Ukraine's folk culture
and sought to advance Ukrainian nationalism, it was heavily persecuted
by the Soviet Union. After Germany invaded and occupied Ukraine in 1941,

Ukrainian Bandurist Chorus of Detroit, circa 1958. (COURTESY OF UKRAINIAN AMERICAN ARCHIVES AND MUSEUM. USED WITH PERMISSION.)

the chorus performed until the occupiers realized it, like Stepan Bandera's OUN, increased the audiences' love of all things "Ukrainian." The chorus was then forced to go to Germany, where it served as slave labor. Eventually, the players, singers, and composers entertained Ukrainian laborers in various camps, where performances helped sustain the internees' love of Ukraine and hope for survival. The Germans permitted the chorus to return to Ukraine for a brief time in 1944 before the Soviets reconquered Ukrainian territory. To escape the Soviets, the chorus once again traveled to Germany and found its way at war's end to a refugee camp in the American zone of occupation. The ensemble re-formed in displaced-person camps in West Germany and Austria and toured Western Europe after the war. In 1949, through the efforts of the Ukrainian American Relief organization, John Panchuk, and Mary Beck, members were able to join the third-wave Ukrainian immigration to the United States and Canada, with Detroit becoming the reconstituted chorus's headquarters. Like all immigrants, chorus members worked in many different fields to establish themselves in North America. The ensemble and the artistic and nationalistic fortitude and beauty it represents persist to this day. The chorus has toured worldwide many times.[102]

Additional Detroit and Michigan Ukrainian groups, businesses, and organizations include the following:[103]

Sports Clubs

- Ukrainian Sports Club "Chernyk"
- Ukrainian Soccer Team "Hoverla"
- Ukrainian Boxing Club

Arts and Cultural Organizations and Associations

- Ukrainian-American Cultural Foundation in Detroit
- Echoes of Ukraine Dance Group
- Ukrainian Cultural Community Club of Detroit
- The Shevchenko Scientific Society, Detroit Chapter
- Ukrainian National Archives and Documentation Center
- Kolomeyka Dancers

Media and Information

- *Detroitski Novyny*
- *Ukrainsky Visti*

Youth Organizations

- Federation of Ukrainian Democratic Youth, Detroit Chapter
- Ukrainian Youth Association of America
- ODUM, Ukrainian Democratic Youth Organization
- SUM (Ukrainian Youth Association)

Civic Groups

- Ukrainian American Civic Committee of Metropolitan Detroit
- "New Wave"
- Ukrainian American Coordinating Council-Detroit Metropolitan Branch
- Ukrainian American Veterans (UAV) Michigan Post 101
- Ukrainian Veterans of World War II
- Ukrainian Children's Aid and Relief Effort (UCARE)

Professional Associations

- Ukrainian-American Chamber of Commerce, Michigan
- American Ukrainian Medical Foundation (AUMF)

Credit Unions

- Ukrainian Future Credit Union (now Selfreliance Federal Credit Union, Chicago)

Ukrainian Intracity Migration

While third-wave Ukrainians energized Detroit's Ukrainian community, they arrived in the city at an inauspicious time. White and non-white populations in Detroit had long been in competition for jobs and housing. The World Wars had increased industrial demand at the same time they decreased immigration and the available workforce. Increased opportunity drew both Southern whites and African Americans to the city in dramatic numbers. Southern whites brought not only their ambition, but also their prejudices, desire for segregation, and beliefs in white Protestant supremacy. Terror groups like the Ku Klux Klan and Black Legion fed on a resurgent nativistic paranoia. These groups were not a cause of unrest but "symptomatic of resentment and fear on the part of a certain class of whites, a resentment which [in addition to African Americans] applied to Catholics, Jews, and the foreign-born."[104] Housing became the flashpoint, which by 1941 "had become intolerable . . . for African-Americans were crowded into segregated areas where they were forced to live under indescribable conditions and were victimized by rapacious landlords."[105] Increasing racialized disparities in space, income, social mobility, and housing quality all helped bring on Detroit's well-documented riots and destruction in 1943 and 1967.

Detroit's Ukrainians—under pressure themselves by nativistic whites for their orthodox religious beliefs and ties to immigration—had to compete for wealth in changing opportunity structures. The post-World War II era witnessed the contraction of the automobile industry and the moving of employment sites to the suburbs, other regions of the United States, and, eventually, other countries. Adding to Ukrainian Americans' employment challenges were anxieties over property values (then, as now, a primary source of private wealth) and the deterioration of their old inner-city neighborhoods. The Ukrainian toehold in the middle class was threatened. These factors prompted many Ukrainians to move out of their old neighborhoods and participate in suburbanization, the "flight" open to them but not at that time to African Americans. Zunz observes that class, rather than ethnic identification, "gradually became a salient feature of urban life . . . [when] the traditional ethnic matrix for people's lives vanished."[106] It is arguable, however, that the "ethnic matrix" vanished because of class, *not* as a precondition for class's dominance of the social order. In other words, the old ethnic neighborhoods on Detroit's west and east side "became increasingly segmented along class lines . . . [and the] white immigrant worker, insecure about his own status in a changing socioethnic hierarchy . . . made every effort to differentiate himself from those he considered to be the lumpenproletariat [poorer whites, newer immigrants, and people of color]."[107] *Differentiation* is just an alternate term for the successful (and anxious) ethnic family relocating from its "working-class neighborhoods for a better life elsewhere in the new urban order."[108]

This differentiation offers the simplest explanation of "the white flight." The causes and effects, however, are likely to be even more complex than ethnic solidarity and class-based segmentation. Perhaps, the old expression that "blood is thicker than water" does not apply to modern and contemporary ethnic communities in the crucible of economic necessity and competition, especially as these communities are made up of increasingly assimilable members. In fact, Robert D. Putnam would argue that all people acquire (and require) "social capital" of two varieties, "bonding" and "bridging."[109] Bonding is "blood," or, to use Putnam's metaphor, a kind of "superglue."[110] Bonding groups are "inward looking and tend to reinforce exclusive [ethnic and nationalistic] identities."[111] They stick together. Almost any of the Michigan Ukrainian groups in the Federation—those based first upon ethnic identification—would qualify. Bridging is "water." Putnam calls it "sociological WD-40."[112] Bridging unsticks; it lubricates. Bridging social capital invigorates the efforts of groups or networks that "are outward looking and encompass people across diverse social cleavages."[113] The crux, as Putnam explains, is that bonding social capital "is good for undergirding specific reciprocity and mobilizing solidarity . . . [and] crucial social and psychological support" for anyone struggling for his or her sustenance in a new, complex, and hypercompetitive environment.[114] However, bridging social capital provides "linkage to external assets."[115] The upshot, Putnam points out (quoting Xavier de Souza Briggs), is that bonding is needed for "getting by," a preoccupation of new immigrants, while bridging is more effective for "getting ahead," even if getting ahead—segmenting, giving in to class and competitive pressures, even to the anxieties attending wealth preservation—meant "getting out," as was the case for assimilating inner-city Ukrainian Michiganders.[116] Ukrainians at first transferred their bonding to specific suburbs, but in the process have gradually bridged, dispersed, assimilated, and followed education, jobs, and marriages (outside the Ukrainian community). Zunz observes that today, "as one drives on Detroit's intracity highways, one cannot avoid being struck by the many churches that stand alone at their intersections, without houses around them. They are the archaeological traces of Detroit's formerly tight [well-bonded] ethnic communities."[117]

Warren, Dearborn, and Dearborn Heights were the first communities to attract Ukrainian groups, to which the new Ukrainian parishes and the Ryan Road community center in these suburbs attest. After all, bonding is never completely replaced. This migration, and the deliberate blocking of some neighborhoods and suburbs (in particular, Warren and Dearborn) to people of color, appear to be motivated more by nativistic ideas of identity than class. Racial exclusion was an overspending of bonding social capital, so to speak, in an effort to preserve not only private wealth but also an idea of America more like the monoracial old country than the multiracial and multiethnic America that Ukrainians had joined and helped build.[118] That Michigan's Ukrainians—themselves victims of active repression both in their own region of Europe and in the United States—were not more empathetic concerning African Americans and their economic and social struggles is an irony uncomfortable for most of Michigan's Ukrainians to consider. Both Ukrainians and African Americans, after all, have been the targets of nativists. As Zunz's observation about isolated churches suggests, the effect of "the white flight" was also deleterious to Ukrainians whose old neighborhoods and churches, now subject to urban blight, were repopulated by other minorities and immigrant groups while Ukrainians and their organizations and parishes lost cohesion and membership. In a competitive society where individualistic wealth and ambition are extolled and rewarded, getting ahead outscores getting by every time. The original ethnic residential enclaves of Ukrainians on the near west and near east sides have almost ceased to exist. The new suburban communities—fragmented by the forces of assimilation and necessity—are not as inclusive as the old immigrant neighborhoods settled by first- and second-wave Ukrainians.

Although dispersed among numerous suburbs, Detroit's Ukrainian American community persists, at least when one looks at the numbers. Thirty-three thousand people in Detroit and its suburbs acknowledge Ukrainian ancestry or cite Ukraine as their place of birth.[119] The manufacturing sector's opportunity structure in the Detroit metro area created during the decades of the first-wave immigration (1870–1914) ensured that the region encompassing Detroit, Hamtramck, Highland Park, and, ultimately, Dearborn, Dearborn Heights, Warren, and Sterling Heights would carry on as one concentration of the Ukrainian diaspora in the United States. Carefully gathered and invested social capital has created and preserved the Ukrainian immigrant community's parishes, schools, mutual aid and fraternal societies, community centers, and a museum and archives, as well as the many sacred and secular social, arts, and service clubs. All together, these institutions and organizations have established and sustained durable (if somewhat stretched and reorganized) network lines for further immigration to the Detroit area. Ukrainians, however, have come not only to the Motor City. All four waves of immigrants have also explored Michigan's other regions and opportunity structures.

CHAPTER THREE

Beyond Metro-Detroit

I t would be difficult to overstate the importance of Detroit's manufacturing and commercial bases to the growth and sustenance of Michigan's Ukrainian community. Still, not all Ukrainians settled in or stayed in Detroit. In 1936, near the end of the second wave of Ukrainian immigration, Wasyl Halich could list thirteen communities outside of Metro-Detroit, Dearborn, and Hamtramck as containing what he considered to be significant clusters of Ukrainians and their descendants: Bay City, Copemish, Flint, Fosters, Fruitport, Grand Rapids, Ironwood, Lansing, Muskegon, Muskegon Heights, Pinconning, Saginaw, and Saline.[1] These Michigan communities have profited from Ukrainian contributions and participation. Table 3 shows the top 30 Michigan municipalities ranked according to Ukrainian population as a percentage of total population.

Noteworthy communities, organizations, and parishes beyond Detroit are described in the following pages.

Ironwood and Farming Communities

According to both Russell M. Magnaghi and Wasyl Halich, Ironwood is the home to a small cluster of Ukrainians (Ruthenians from Western Ukraine) brought there for iron and copper mining.[2] Halich remarks that agriculture

RANK	CITY	POPULATION	PERCENTAGE OF TOTAL
1	Oakland	4,180	2.86%
2	Topinabee	68	2.15%
3	Hamtramck	46,136	2.13%
4	Whittaker	106	2.11%
5	Willis	2,616	1.86%
6	Glen Arbor	554	1.76%
7	Sterling	2,755	1.51%
8	Warren	138,152	1.47%
9	Somerset	555	1.45%
10	Center Line	8,789	1.42%
11	Dearborn Heights	58,248	1.36%
12	Owendale	1,011	1.34%
13	Oak Park	32,493	1.30%
14	Beaver Island	551	1.28%
15	Port Sanilac	1,457	1.28%
16	Fulton	850	1.25%
17	Lennon	3,807	1.22%
18	Troy	80,966	1.21%
19	Onondaga	1,871	1.15%
20	Douglas	740	1.13%
21	Henderson	860	1.12%
22	Livonia	100,767	1.07%
23	Alden	1,101	1.07%
24	Onsted	4,828	1.06%
25	Oakley	1,759	1.05%
26	West Bloomfield	66,214	1.04%
27	Au Train	570	1.03%
28	Pleasant Ridge	2,384	1.01%
29	Saint Helen	4,525	1.01%
30	Madison Heights	31,101	1.00%

Table 3. Michigan Cities and Ukrainians (or Ukrainian Descent) as Percentage of Total Population.

SOURCE: ZIP ATLAS, "CITIES WITH THE HIGHEST PERCENTAGE OF UKRAINIANS IN MICHIGAN," HTTP://ZIPATLAS.COM/US/MI/CITY-COMPARISON/PERCENTAGE-UKRAINIAN-POPULATION.HTM.

drew Ukrainians to "Copemish, Fruitport, Pinconning, and Saline. Here most of the Ukrainians bought wooded land without buildings and converted it into fruit and corn . . . farms [with] two hundred families living on them."[3]

Ann Arbor

Ann Arbor's Ukrainian community began with two pastors by the names of Baczynsky and Kustodowych, who served a trio of farm families named Kostishak, Hrushewsky, and Kozmiuk.[4] Within the town of Ann Arbor, however, minds were trained and intellects harvested, for this small city was home to no less than the University of Michigan, Concordia University, and Washtenaw Community College, with Eastern Michigan University and Cleary University in neighboring towns. Ann Arbor became an intellectual powerhouse at the same time that immigrant Ukrainians were congregating down the road in the economic powerhouse of Detroit. Professor Stefan Tymoshenko (Stephen Timoshenko), a Ukrainian, chaired the Theoretical Mechanics Department at the University of Michigan until 1936, when the "Father of Theoretical Mechanics" left to create similar departments at the University of California and Stanford.[5] Ukrainians began graduating from the University of Michigan in the early 1900s.[6] The 1920s saw Detroit activist Petro Zaporozhets and respected lawyer and politician Ivan Panchuk receive their degrees.[7] The Ukrainian Students' Club at the University "was organized on December 11, 1951[,] by three students [third-wavers] . . . [named] Mykola Dumyk, Bohdan Nehaniw[,] and Zenko Melnyk."[8] Mirroring the small but active ethnic group whence it came, the club "had only fourteen members [but] . . . quickly became very active and highly visible on the University of Michigan campus."[9] In November 1956, the club was nationally recognized for picketing a Kremlin delegation that "came to observe the American election process."[10] In 1953, as third-wave Ukrainians were acclimating to their new country, Dr. Assya Humesky joined the university. Dr. Humesky championed the Ukrainian Students' Club and, in the 1970s, as the children of the third-wave were looking for culturally relevant programming, began course offerings in Ukrainian culture, literature, and language. More clubs, scholarships, and courses followed.[11] Third-wave families responded to these academic opportunities, as well as to other professional opportunities in the town. The first off-campus community organization was the Ukrainian

National Women's League of America, which sponsored and staffed a "seven class Ukrainian Heritage School for children of Ukrainian descent," which was in operation for ten years.[12] The Ann Arbor Ukrainian community grew until it had representatives not only in the educational organizations in the town, but also in the agricultural, business, and professional ranks.[13]

Jackson

Until being subsumed by the unrelenting forces of assimilation, Ukrainians in the Jackson area of Michigan organized under several ethnic-based organizations. In 1922 Stepan Pylypczuk established a branch of the Ukrainian Workingmen's Association (UWA). This branch, like other UWA branches, was a fraternal mutual aid organization.[14] He and business associates Petro Svoboda and Wasyl Rohach organized "picnics on farms around Jackson, Lansing, Albion[,] and Grand Rapids in order to acquaint other Ukrainians with this organization and register them as members."[15] The more right-leaning Rohach split with Pylypczuk and formed Branch #302 of the Ukrainian National Organization (UNO), which included the Lucyshyn family from Homer, who had struck it rich in the oil business. This UNO branch was joined by third-wave Ukrainians who quickly adopted local Protestant and Russian Orthodox faiths. When Rohach passed away, Andrij Zakala took a leadership position in the UNO, only to watch it decline as the immigrants' children took other (bridging) paths to social acceptance. He admitted that "without their own church as a unifying factor, it has been very difficult to keep the Ukrainian group from being assimilated into American society."[16]

Grand Rapids

Ukrainians in the Grand Rapids area, however, did have their own parish, St. Michael Ukrainian Catholic Church, which uses the "Byzantine Liturgies of St. John Chrysostom and St. Basil the Great."[17] Founded in 1949, during the third wave of Ukrainian immigration, the St. Michael parish was infused with the third-wave refugee spirit of resistance to the Russification and repression in Ukraine after World War II. As recounted by parish authorities,

> Between the years of 1946 and 1991, most of our bishops, priests, and [the] religious of our Church in Ukraine were either killed by the Communists,

St. Michael's Ukrainian Catholic Church, Grand Rapids (COURTESY OF MICHAEL MICHALEK. CROPPED AND RECOLORED TO GRAYSCALE. USED WITH PERMISSION.)

or suffered long prison terms. Those who were not killed were forced to practice their faith in hiding. Cognizant of this fact, we are a church which knows the true value of our religion . . . and practices our faith with fervor and devotion.[18]

The parishioners write of their intent "to retain a little of the Ukrainian language in a few parts of our liturgy . . . This helps us maintain a link with our past and remember our saintly forefathers from whom we received the Faith."[19]

Jacob's Falls

Since 1983, in Michigan's upper peninsula, at Jacob's Falls on Michigan's Keweenaw Peninsula, there has been a Ukrainian Catholic monastery associated with the Skete society of monks of the Holy Protection. In their own words, they are "a Catholic Monastery of the Byzantine rite, under the jurisdiction of The Ukrainian Catholic Eparchy of St. Nicholas in Chicago."[20] The monks there embrace the arts as forms of spiritual devotion, living according to the orthodox belief that the sacred must embrace the true and beautiful. When the monks first moved to the region, they picked the wild fruit available on the peninsula. Today they operate a fruit and jam business to support their traditional monastic calling. The monks write, "Monasteries exist for the salvation of the monks and to lead others to holiness and the kingdom of God."[21]

Flint

Owing to Flint's opportunity structure, the Ukrainian community there followed the settlement pattern already established in Detroit. As in Detroit, first-wave immigrants arrived in Flint in the last quarter of the nineteenth century from "the regions of Halychyna, Lemkiwshchyna[,] and Transcarpathia [Western Ukraine]," although some had tried "Brazil, Canada[,] or other cities in the United States."[22] These economic opportunity seekers first worked as farmers and laborers, but as industry opened, they moved to the factories of General Motors or its suppliers. Like first-wave Ukrainians in Detroit's inner city, those in Flint soon established a community center: "A group of the more nationally and socially aware Ukrainian immigrants joined together to buy a meeting house . . . they named the 'Ukrainian American Community Club.'"[23] Once this toehold was established, the Club provided support for a branch of the Ukrainian Workingmen's Association, which, as has been described, has branches in Detroit, Jackson, and other communities. This mutual aid society also served second-wave workers and their families as they arrived.

When third-wave immigrants began to arrive in the early 1950s, "the charter of the 'Ukrainian American Club' was changed, as was its name, to the 'Ivan Franko Ukrainian Home Association.'"[24] Energized by these refugee Ukrainians, the community organized a Catholic parish, Saint Vladimir Ukrainian Catholic Church, using space in "the Home" until a church building could be purchased. The Home Association also hosted a branch of "the Ukrainian Congress Committee, a branch of the Ukrainian National Association, a chapter of the Ukrainian National Women's League of America, and the Flint Branch of the Ukrainian Youth Association of America."[25] Once St. Vladimir's got its own building in 1952, a chapter of the Providence Association of Ukrainian Catholics in America was added to this ambitious parish's roster of mutual aid and cultural organizations.

According to Stepan Stefaniw, Wolodymyr Pytlowanyj, and Nicholas Bartkiw, the 1960s was a prosperous decade for Flint's Ukrainians. Members of the Home association built a new building, and the influence of this new addition to the community provided impetus for a "teen division of the Ukrainian Youth Association of America."[26] Named "'Mukachiv,' [the group] was organized and a branch of [the] Ukrainian National Aid Association was also formed."[27] Saint Vladimir's acquired a new parish house and it quickly "became the focal point of the community's religious life and also the site of a school of Ukrainian language and religion."[28]

Saginaw

Saginaw's Western Ukrainians (from "Ternopil, Zbarazh, Horodenka, Turka[,] and Rudky") began to settle in the Saginaw area in 1919–1920, during the second wave of Ukrainian immigration.[29] These immigrants worked primarily in the region's steel mills. Like Detroit and Flint, Saginaw came to host a branch of the Ukrainian National Association. In 1924, Ivan Kinash, Oleksa Varian, and Hryohorij Fedus organized the "Ukrainian Club Society," sponsored by Branch #300 of the Ukrainian National Association. All worked to establish Holy Trinity Ukrainian Orthodox parish (now closed). The club met in the local Lithuanian Hall, and "by 1954, this Branch had fifty-two adult and juvenile members."[30]

Muskegon Heights

Like Saginaw, Muskegon Heights supported a small group of Ukrainian families in which the fathers labored in the steel and wood products industries. This group had immigrated "from Sambir, Dolyna[,] and Peremyshi [in] western Ukraine in 1909–1910," the waning years of the first wave.[31] For six decades Ukrainians maintained the St. Nicholas Ukrainian Catholic church in Muskegon Heights, eventually moving from a temporary setting into what was once a Polish church on Park Street.[32] Associated with the parish was Branch #131 (Prosvita Society) of the Ukrainian National Association, which was organized in 1918 during the interwar period.[33] The Prosvita group contributed much to amateur theatricals in the town and "to many Ukrainian causes in the United States and in Ukraine."[34] St. Nicholas also sponsored a small Ridna Shkola (heritage school) and an active branch of the Sisterhood of St. Ann (Branch #187 of the Providence Association of Ukrainian Catholics in America). The sisterhood worked to maintain the parish. The diligence of Fathers Holowaty and Solomon was not enough, however, to stave off the loss of parishioners to the Protestant, Roman Catholic, and American Orthodox competition. The Sisterhood was dissolved in the 1970s, and St. Nicholas closed as well. The building still exists and has been leased by the Ukrainian Catholic Eparchy of Chicago to Muslims for an Islamic Educational Center.

Traverse City

In 1991, with the collapse of the USSR, Ukraine won its long-sought-after independence. Since that time and continuing today, 500 fourth-wave Ukrainian Protestant refugees and their families have emigrated to the Traverse City area. These families can thank the First Congregational Church, Traverse City Central United Methodist Church, the Church of Philadelphia in Traverse City, and New Hope Community Church for offering a haven from post-Soviet religious persecution. First Congregational and Central United Methodist are the primary sponsors and have continued to support their Ukrainian parishioners.[35] Recently, these churches have supported Ukrainians who are fleeing the Russian invasions of the Donbas region and Crimean peninsula.[36] The congregations are also educating the local community about this new war and holding fundraisers for Ukrainians who arrive with little or nothing, much as third-wave refugees did in the late 1940s and early 1950s.[37] The churches offer selective services in English, Russian, and Ukrainian since the Ukrainian population in Traverse City speaks all three languages.[38]

Like other ethnic groups, Michigan's Ukrainians have been encouraged by the state's generosity, diverse opportunity structures, regional variety, and established immigrant communities spreading from its southeast to its northwest. Recent refugees from economic, military, political, and religious upheavals in the homeland are still finding sympathetic networks of sponsors as they establish themselves socially and economically.

Traditional Cultural Practices of Michigan's Ukrainians

Regardless of the region of origin, specific Michigan destination, and degree of assimilation, Michigan's Ukrainians have customs that help them bond and remain "Ukrainian." In their own ways, clothing, jewelry, cuisine, liquors, celebrations, educational practices, and cultural expression help establish and sustain the Old World identity of Ukrainian Michiganders.

Traditional Clothing

At the most celebratory times of the year, it is easy to spot Ukrainians in a multiethnic Michigan, for they often wear either traditional Ukrainian clothing or elements thereof. Traditional outfits are very elaborate, with different versions depending on the wearer's age and social status, as well as on the occasion, season, and region of origin.[1] Each set of clothes has a wide variety of elements starting with underclothing, shirts, gowns, pants, belts, vests, head scarves, head crowns, and outerwear. All elements are designed to be decorative and functional at the same time. The attention to detail and quality of the fabrics are highly valued. The most typical traditional clothing among Ukrainians in Michigan are embroidered gowns (sorochka, pronounced soh-ROCH-kah), embroidered shirts (vyshyvanka, pronounced vyh-shyh-VAHN-kah, for men and women), and traditional necklaces for

Ukrainian Jewelry. Layers of coral necklaces with silver beads. Choker on a ribbon with coin mounted on silver. (COURTESY OF ANDRIY PASLAVSKY, JEWELRY STUDIO VYDYMO-NEVYDYMO. USED WITH PERMISSION.)

women. It was typical for Ukrainians of the first and second waves to bring the traditional clothing with them. They worked very hard to preserve it and replicate it with the help of local designers, thus creating a unique collection of traditional Ukrainian clothing in the United States. Traditional clothing is worn to special celebrations at church (Christmas and Easter Masses, weddings, and baptisms) and prominent public events (school assemblies and formal cultural celebrations). These clothing items can easily be purchased online, which allows Michiganders to wear authentic traditional clothing if they wish. Evidence of such clothing can be found in many of the photos in this book.

One of the staples of a Ukrainian woman's apparel is her jewelry. As in Ukraine, Michigan's first- and second-wave immigrants use jewelry not only to indicate social status but also to ensure good fortune and protection from evil spirits. Ukrainian women primarily value coral as a necklace material, even though garnet, amber, pearls, glass beads, and ceramic beads also have been popular.[2] Coral necklaces can be very expensive. The necklaces often have coins (gold and silver; Austrian, Polish, and Russian) and crosses to make them even more impressive. Women often wear multiple rows of different necklaces, chokers, and chains for special occasions. When Ukrainian Michiganders get together, this jewelry is still displayed and coveted.

Traditional Cuisine and Drinks

Ukrainians have always taken great pride in and put great effort into preparing homemade foods. Many Michigan-Ukrainian households eat freshly made foods every day. As Marta Pisetska Farley explains,

> Ukrainians took food seriously. Its symbolism, preparation, and consumption were important . . . At large feasts, the hosts saw to the needs of the guests, and sometimes stood and hovered over them . . . [T]he host's duty was to encourage guests to eat more. This encouragement and demurral went on, back and forth, until everyone was very full . . . After the meal, each guest and family member thanked the host for the repast.[3]

Because Ukrainians use only fresh produce, their cuisine changes with the season and region. Not surprisingly, border areas were influenced by the distinctive cuisines of Ukraine's neighbors, the Russian Federation, Poland,

Borscht

There are many recipes for borscht. The majority will have matchstick-cut beets (or beet stock), shredded cabbage, and beans (cannellini and other varieties of white beans are the most common). Since these three ingredients take longest to cook, they are simmered for an hour before adding other ingredients. In its simplest form, borscht is a vegetable soup made with beets, cabbage, sautéed onions, match-cut carrots, cubed potatoes, crushed tomatoes or tomato paste, and fresh or dried parsley and dill. The vegan version can be made during the fasting times and will be served with crushed or minced garlic, fresh chives if available, and bread. If the season does not require fasting, borscht will be served with sour cream in addition to garlic and chives. The more complicated recipes are made with different stocks (bone, vegetable) and different types of meats and mushrooms. Often, each household will have its unique borscht that will be proudly served throughout the year. The recipes are versatile and accommodate different diets.

Belarus, Slovakia, Hungary, Romania, and Moldova. For example, one can find many Hungarian dishes in Transcarpathia and Polish dishes in northwestern Ukraine. Many international dishes were brought to Ukraine during the Soviet times, when ingredients from different republics were introduced. Ukrainian cuisine has also been influenced by Jewish cuisine, since Ukraine has always had a significant Jewish population and Jews have often owned taverns.

Because the various waves of immigrants arrived from every region of the old country, a wide selection of Ukraine's cuisines has found its way to Michigan. Some of the staples of Ukrainian cuisine seen in Michigan homes are borscht (beet soup), holubtsi (stuffed cabbage), varenyky (dumplings), kapusniak (sauerkraut soup), kyshka (buckwheat and blood sausage), medivnyk (honey torte), pyrizhky (hand pies), and nalysnyky (crepes).

Each wave of Ukrainian immigration to Michigan brought its own selection of dishes. Also, differences in social class enriched the variety of each region. Simple people tended to eat simple foods and used their own gardens to supplement their diet, pickling the surplus for winter sustenance.

Wealthier people had more options and could enjoy whatever the culture offered. Gradually, recipes were adapted to a new American lifestyle. For example, the American tradition of cookie baking and exchanges was adopted by the Ukrainian community even though there is no such tradition in Ukraine. However, Ukrainian recipes for cookies and pastry were used instead of American ones. Since the number of immigrants has been large and their connections across the Upper Midwest have been well established, the exchange of cookbooks and adapted recipes—whatever is familiar and cherished by each wave of immigration—has been active.

Recipe sharing, however, has undergone a curious reversal. Because many recipes lost to the homeland have been preserved here by immigrant families, researchers from the old country now visit Michigan to learn about their Ukrainian past. As researcher Marianna Dushar points out, the first two waves of Ukrainian immigrants preserved regional dishes that have all but disappeared in contemporary Ukraine. Ukrainian American cuisine, therefore, has had an important archival function, preserving both Ukrainian heritage and identity.[4]

There seems to be no lack of venues for traditional foods. Ukrainians in Michigan can treat themselves to Ukrainian dishes at the Ukrainian Cultural Center in Warren, Michigan, or cater their foods from women who run catering businesses from their homes. There are also ethnic delis in the Detroit area that offer an array of Ukrainian, Polish, and Russian dishes and delicacies. The cuisine has also become the main instrument of fundraising for Ukrainian parishes. The causes needing support might be in Michigan or the homeland.

Ukrainians also have their own national liquors. One of the most well-known and distinctive is horilka (hoh-REEHL-kah), a clear distilled alcoholic beverage traditionally made of sugar beets. Honey, pepper, herbs, and berries can be used to make flavored horilka. This beverage is a staple of Ukrainian celebrations and is not mixed but consumed in one- or two-ounce "shots" when toasting, a practice that for non-Ukrainians seems elaborate, endless, and punishing. Horilka is imported from Ukraine and is widely available at Michigan's ethnic stores. Other types of fruit and sweet liquors, wine, and beer are also popular among Ukrainian immigrants.

Paska (COURTESY OF TORANGE.BIZ. CROPPED AND RECOLORED TO GRAYSCALE. USED WITH PERMISSION.)

Bread

Ukraine is famous for its breads. Owing to its fertile soil, mild climate, and long growing season, Ukraine has been called (and coveted as) the Breadbasket of Europe. The appreciation for wheat (the main grain for flour in Ukraine) is reflected in the Ukrainian flag, where "wide horizontal blue and yellow stripes call up a picture of fair blue skies above abundant gold fields of grain."[*] The ingredients, flours, and techniques (yeast and different types of sourdough) vary. Bread makers are well respected in Ukraine since bread-making requires skill, experience, and physical strength. Breads were used in rituals in pre-Christian times and were adopted by many Christian practices. Breads still function centrally in secular and sacred rituals such as weddings, engagements, baptisms, funerals, memorials, spring welcoming, and major religious holidays. When visiting someone's house for the first time, it is customary to bring a loaf of bread as a wish for good health and prosperity. Ukraine has always grown a wide variety of grains that could be milled and used in breads. Traditionally, whole grain varieties were used in everyday baking, while enriched and bleached flours were reserved for holidays and special occasions.

Paska (pronounced PAHS-kah) is Ukraine's ritualistic Easter bread. Paska is a rich yeast bread in the shape of a cylinder, and there are many different recipes that change according to the region of origin. The bread is baked on the Thursday or Saturday before Easter and has been a staple of the Easter feast for centuries. In general, a loaf of paska is a sweet, thick column of bread made with bleached flour and rich with eggs or egg yolks. The top of the bread can be covered with egg wash or can be decorated with different types of glazes, frostings, or sprinkles. Some paskas have tops decorated with different dough cut-outs in the shape of crosses, leaves, and braids. Like other yeast breads, paska has to be kneaded thoroughly for the dough to be elastic, and the dough requires two or three risings. Simple recipes will include eggs, butter (or sunflower oil), milk, yeast, and flour. More sophisticated recipes will feature rum, blends of spices, almond and vanilla extracts, dried or candied fruit (raisins are common), and chocolate bits.[†]

---

[*] "Christmas in Ukraine," *Christmas Around the World from World Book* (Chicago: World, 1997), 41.
[†] Maryna Hedeen, personal interview, July 6, 2020.

Selyansky (peasant bread) (COURTESY OF VALENTYA VZDULSKA. CROPPED AND RECOLORED TO GRAYSCALE. USED WITH PERMISSION.)

Varenyky with potato filling and bacon (COURTESY OF KAGOR. CROPPED AND RECOLORED TO GRAYSCALE. USED WITH PERMISSION.)

Varenyky

Varenyky* (stuffed dumplings) are popular in Ukrainian cuisine for their versatility. They can be sweet and served as a dessert, or they can be salty and served as a main dish. The simple dough for varenyky is made with water and flour. The dough is kneaded until it is smooth and elastic. Small circles are cut out of a flat sheet of this dough, and a teaspoon of filling is placed in the center of the circle. Then the circle is folded in half, and a "W" shape is made with the thumb, index, and middle fingers on one of the ends. The "W" is sealed with the fingers, and the fold along the edge is pinched together. Another "W" seals the other end of the crescent shaped dumpling.

Since the dough for varenyky is neither sweet nor salty, the fillings define how to serve them. Sweet fillings include berries (raspberries, strawberries, wild strawberries, or blueberries), cherries (sweet and tart), prunes, and poppy seeds. Varenyky with sweet fillings are often served in sugar syrup or are rolled in sugar. Some of the salty fillings include mashed potatoes, farmers cheese, salty cheeses (like feta), ground meat, liver, sauerkraut, and mushrooms.

After varenyky are filled and sealed, they are cooked in boiling water until they float to the top. The water is then drained, and a pile of the stuffed dumplings is served hot with oil, butter, or lard, depending on the season. During fasting times, Ukrainians make vegan versions served with onions sautéed in sunflower oil. During other times, varenyky can be served with bacon bits, butter, sour cream, and fresh parsley and dill.

* *Varenyk* is a singular noun pronounced as Vah-REH-nyk with the stress pronounced on the second syllable; *varenyky* is a plural noun pronounced as Vah-REH-nyh-kyh.

Celebrations

Michigan's Ukrainians love festivities and are known for their hospitality and elaborate feasts, usually on religious and secular holidays. Different holidays are associated with different culinary traditions. Often ethnographers talk about Ukrainian holidays as pauses in a journey lasting a calendar year. Kateryna Mischenko—researcher at the National Center of Folk Art "Ivan Honchar Museum" in Kyiv—lists twelve holidays that are typically celebrated throughout the Ukrainian world. They are Christmas (December 25 or January 6), Saint Basil or the Old New Year (January 14), Epiphany (January 19), Shrove Tuesday (varies), Easter (varies), Pentecost (varies), Summer Solstice (June 7 or 21), Harvest Festivals, the Feast of Transfiguration, the Feast of the Protection of Our Most Holy Lady (October 14), Apostle Andrew Day (December 12), and Saint Nickolas Day (December 6 or 19).[5] These celebrations have established traditions and often are observed by Michigan's Ukrainians. The most important cycle of holidays is the Christmas or winter cycle, which begins with Apostle Andrew Day on December 12 and ends with Epiphany on January 19 (dates are based on the Julian calendar). Unlike other Christians, Ukrainians have a very festive Advent season full of folk traditions and celebrations interwoven into religious holidays.

Ukrainians in Michigan most often celebrate Saint Nickolas Day, Christmas, Easter, and Summer Solstice. Specific celebrations will depend on the wave of immigration and region of origin. Recently, the Feast of the Protection of Our Most Holy Lady has become a popular fundraising day for the Ukrainian army since the same date (October 14) has also been designated as Defender of Ukraine Day across the Ukrainian world.[6]

Reflecting the ancient influences on Ukrainian religion, Ukrainians have preserved many pagan traditions and blended them with the Christian ones: "Ancient Ukrainian peoples worshipped the sun god . . . The agricultural cycle, which is naturally aligned with the changing position of the sun, is the central focus of many age-old Ukrainian religious traditions . . . Work, play, and worship are all tightly interwoven in the daily life of Ukrainians."[7] While many of Michigan's Ukrainians may not be aware of the pagan origins of some celebrations and traditions, they observe them nevertheless as a part of their own folk culture. These pagan traditions are an organic component of Ukraine's rich and unique Christian celebrations. For example, there are many pagan carols that became part of Ukraine's caroling tradition and are sung in Ukraine and across the Ukrainian world. Many of these carols refer to the sun, moon, and stars as divine; reveal nature's sacredness through its blessings (rain, harvest) and curses (droughts, floods); ask ancient gods for prosperity and bountiful harvests; glorify family life; praise the wisdom of the head of the family and the beauty of the family's women; and give thanks for the wealth of the family.[8]

Another interesting example of such blending of pagan and Christian traditions among Michigan's Ukrainians can be found in Easter egg decorating. Eggs are a symbol of rebirth in many pagan cultures and have become an Easter symbol around the globe. Ukrainians adapted this pagan symbol to a Christian holiday, and thus pysanka dyeing (PYH-sahn-kah) was born. A decorated egg is a powerful talisman against evil spirits, for it is decorated with symbols of fertility, prosperity, beauty, and other Slavic virtues. Both the Ukrainian American Archives and Museum and Detroit's Institute of Arts have large collections of pysanky made by Michiganders.

One of the most vibrant Christian adaptations of a pagan holiday is the Summer Solstice, or Ivan Kupala festival, celebrated on June 21 or July 7. In pagan tradition, the holiday was a celebration of fertility, earthly love, and spiritual cleansing. The cleansing was associated with jumping over bonfires: "Participants danced, decorated trees, placed wreaths on the water, and created effigies of Slavic gods."[9] Later, these festivities became a part of the John the Baptist celebration, which allowed Ukrainians to continue to celebrate the festival near water. In Michigan, Detroit's New Wave organization holds yearly Ivana Kupala, or Summer Solstice, celebrations.[10]

Michigan's Ukrainians also enjoy a rich tradition of secular celebrations, which are typically for friends and family and feature special dishes (traditional Ukrainian or international) and multiple rounds of drinks. The immigrant wave to which a Ukrainian family belongs might influence the importance and customs surrounding a particular celebration. For example, according to Olga Kari, the New Year has become the most important secular holiday for fourth-wave and recent Ukrainians who enjoy large parties, fireworks, gift exchanges, and Christmas trees.[11] In Soviet times, a Christmas tree was called a New Year tree and was decorated at the end of December. The gifts were placed under the tree and distributed on New Year's Eve or Day. There was a Soviet version of Santa, Grandpa Frost (*Did Moroz*, pronounced Deed Moh-ROH-z), who was accompanied by his granddaughter Snihuronka (pronounced Sneeh-HUH-rohn-kah) and brought presents to children at home, day care centers, and schools. That said, many immigrants will have assimilated and switched to decorating Christmas trees at the beginning of December, giving gifts on Christmas morning, and including the figure of Santa Claus like most Americans. Giving gifts on Christmas

Pysanky (COURTESY OF UKRAINIAN AMERICAN ARCHIVES AND MUSEUM. COURTESY OF MARYNA HEDEEN. CROPPED AND RECOLORED TO GRAYSCALE. © MARYNA HEDEEN. USED WITH PERMISSION.)

Learning how to make pysanky, circa 1950 (COURTESY OF UKRAINIAN AMERICAN ARCHIVES AND MUSEUM. CROPPED AND RECOLORED TO GRAYSCALE. USED WITH PERMISSION.)

Pysanky

Pysanky are elaborately dyed and decorated eggs and are a staple for Ukraine's Easter holidays.* Each region in Ukraine has its own patterns and techniques for decorating the eggs. In general, a pysanka (preferably hollow) is dyed multiple times in different food colorings or natural dyes. Melted beeswax is applied in a pattern or design before each dyeing. The wax protects the shell from coloring, and multiple waxings and dyeings create elaborate patterns. At the end of each dyeing cycle, the wax is removed by heating the egg above a candle.

Around Easter time, there are many workshops at churches, parochial schools, and cultural centers on how to make pysanky. For example, the Polish Center in Hamtramck holds annual workshops for those interested in learning this popular folk art. The center also sells the tools necessary to make pysanky at home. There are pysanka artists in Michigan who make pysanky for show and sale. For example, Roman Seniuk was well known in the Detroit Metro area for his pysanky workshops and exhibits. His earliest memory of pysanky was seeing the intricately decorated eggs on Easter Sunday at his church. "They were the most beautiful things he had ever seen, so his mother helped him learn how to make pysanky himself from various kinds of eggs, beeswax, a kistka stylus, a candle, and dyes."[†] Seniuk graduated from Saginaw Valley State College in Saginaw, Michigan, with a BS in fine arts, specializing in design and illustration. After the artist died, some of his works were donated to the Ukrainian American Archives and Museum in Hamtramck. There are also private collectors in Michigan who have extended collections of pysanky, not only from Ukraine but also from other Eastern European countries. Their collections are often on loan to local museums and cultural centers. Pysanky made by Dr. Luba Petrusha are on loan to the Ukrainian American Archives and Museum.[‡] The Detroit Institute of Art also has an extensive collection of Ukrainian pysanky, which are referred to as "Easter Eggs" in the museum collection.[§]

* Pysanka is a singular noun pronounced as PYH-san-ka with a stress on the first syllable; pysanky is a plural noun pronounced as PYH-san-kyh.
† Roman Seniuk, "Pysanky by Roman Seniuk," http://romanseniuk.tripod.com.
‡ "Pysanky from the Chernihiv Region," Ukrainian American Archives and Museum, Ukrainian Museum, May 11, 2020.
§ "Easter Eggs," Detroit Institute of Art, https://www.dia.org/art/collection/object/easter-eggs-30243?page=1.

Christmas Crafts

Ukrainians have traditional Christmas decorative crafts that are made or purchased every year. The first one is a geometrical mobile made of straws that is
supposed to resemble a spider and is called a pavuk (pronounced pah-VUHK),
which means spider in Ukrainian.* The pavuk is hung from the ceiling and sym-
bolizes the creation of the world. The second is a sheath of wheat and dried
flowers called didukh† (DEEH-duh). The didukh is a symbol of ancestors and
family prosperity. The last one is an octagonal star called a zirka (pronounced
ZIHR-kah), which is carried by carolers when they visit houses.‡ The zirka is a
symbol of the Star of Bethlehem and a pre-Christian symbol of the sun at the
beginning of a new calendar year. These decorative crafts are made by professional crafters and can be purchased online. Also, schoolchildren at Ridna
Shkola and Ukrainian parochial schools make them as a part of their Christmas
celebrations.

* Kateryna Mischenko, "Ukrainian Year: Holidays That Unite Us." National Center of Folk Culture "Ivan Honchar Mu-
seum," https://honchar.org.ua/p/ukrajinskyj-rik-svyata-scho-nas-objednuyut.
† "Christmas in Ukraine." *Christmas Around the World from World Book* (Chicago: World, 1997), 34.
‡ Mischenko, op. cit.

morning, however, may not have prevented parents from preserving their
childhood traditions from Ukraine and allowing their children also to be
visited in early December by Saint Nickolas. These lucky children receive
presents twice during the holiday season.

Ukrainian American Christmas Celebrations

Some Ukrainian Americans follow the Gregorian calendar, celebrating
Christmas on December 25 like their American neighbors. However, others follow the Julian calendar used by the Ukrainian Catholic and Orthodox
churches, which is two weeks behind the Gregorian calendar. These Ukrainians will celebrate Christmas Eve on January 6 and Christmas on January 7.[12]
Ukrainian Christmas is unique because it combines the Christian celebration
of the birth of Jesus with pre-Christian celebrations of creating the world,
paying respects to the deceased, and maintaining balance and harmony.[13]

Kutia (COURTESY OF MARIANNA DUSHAR. CROPPED AND RECOLORED TO GRAYSCALE. USED WITH PERMISSION.)

Regardless of the calendar followed, Christmas Eve and Christmas Day will be celebrated in similar ways. On Christmas Eve, the most magical part of Christmas, the whole family will gather for a special dinner consisting of fasting dishes. According to the tradition, there are twelve fasting dishes to commemorate the twelve full moons of the year and Christianity's twelve apostles.[14] One of these dishes is kutia (pronounced kuh-TIAH), a sweet grain dish served in a bowl. Kutia is a pre-Christian ritualistic dish that is supposed to be shared with the souls of the deceased. Traditionally, it is made with wheat berries, honey, raisins, various nuts, and poppyseeds. Each region of Ukraine has a slightly different recipe for kutia, so Michigan's immigrants from different regions might have different versions of it, but the main ingredient, cooked wheat berries, will be in all of them. Many families will have a fasting version of borscht (beet soup), varenyky (small flour dumplings filled with vegetables and fruit), pickled herring or other fish dishes, mushrooms, dill pickles, sauerkraut or potato dishes, a vegan version of holubtsi (stuffed

Christmas Carols

Kolyadky (pronounced koh-LIAHD-kyh), or Christmas carols, are sung on Christmas Day. Most are religious and glorify the birth of Jesus. Many churches have adult and children's choirs who perform kolyadky during the holidays at churches, schools, and cultural centers. Small vocal ensembles also will visit community members to sing carols in their homes, and these community members will reward the carolers with tips and snacks. Schedrivky (Sh-chehd-RIHV-kyh) are more secular carols and are performed on January 14, Saint Basil's Day. Ukraine's most famous carol is "The Carol of the Bells," a very old, pre-Christian Ukrainian carol that glorifies the head of the household and wishes him a wealthy year with full barns and root cellars.* This carol was arranged in 1916 by Mykola Leontovych, a prominent Ukrainian composer. The song is included in many Christmas collections in North America.

Traditionally, kolyadky and schedrivky were performed on distinct days. However, Ukrainian immigrants, like their North American neighbors, will listen to both throughout the Christmas season. This new tradition shows the assimilation of Ukrainian Michiganders into American culture. The gift shop at the Ukrainian American Archives and Museum of Detroit has vinyl records and CDs of carols performed by the Ukrainian Bandurist Chorus. Michigan's Ukrainians sing carols near the Christmas tree in downtown Detroit, and since 2014, Ukrainians have participated in the international Christmas concert in Southfield, which is organized by the Council of Orthodox Churches of Metropolitan Detroit.[†] The concert features "Nativity hymns and carols from Greece, Romania, Serbia, Ukraine and other lands, sung by selected choirs from churches."[‡]

* "Mykola Leontovych," *Internet Encyclopedia of Ukraine*, http://www.encyclopediaofukraine.com.
† "Orthodox Organization Sponsors Christmas Concert in Southfield," *Morning Sun*, https://www.themorningsun.com/lifestyles/orthodox-organization-sponsors-christmas-concert-in-southfield/article_8a3d0d68-0927-5f1e-a7b4-98b3896dc7b1.html.
‡ Ibid.

cabbage, pronounced hoh-LUHB-tsi), beans, and special breads. The preparation of a Ukrainian style Christmas dinner is lengthy and elaborate and involves different generations of the same family.

The meal will start with a prayer for the souls of the deceased and a spoonful of kutia. Then the rest of the courses will be enjoyed. Many families will leave the remaining food on the table as an offering to the souls of the deceased. Members of the gathered family might wear traditional embroidered clothes to the dinner. Ukrainians believe it is especially important to gather as families on Christmas Eve since this day erases the boundary between present and past by bringing the spirits of ancestors back into the family.

On Christmas Day, the family will gather again for a sumptuous meal of delicious meats and salads. There is no Christmas gift-giving tradition in Ukraine. As mentioned earlier, however, some families may choose to follow the American tradition and give presents on Christmas Day. Others may follow the Soviet-era practice of exchanging gifts on New Year's Eve. Many will send gifts of money or parcels to their families in the old country. Michigan has offices of two main shipping companies to Ukraine, Dnipro LLC and Meest Express. These offices are conveniently located in Warren next to the Ukrainian Cultural Center and are busy all year, with the biggest demand around Christmas and New Year. Starting in October, Ukrainians in Michigan ship various goods (clothes, electronics, toys, vitamins, household goods, etc.) to their family and friends in Ukraine. Ukrainians in Michigan will also receive holiday presents from the homeland. Typically, these include regional foods, sweets, and traditional textiles and embroidery, some of which cannot be purchased in local ethnic or online stores.

Ukrainian American Easter Celebrations

Easter is another important holiday for Michigan's Ukrainian immigrants. As with Christmas, the date depends upon whether a family follows the Gregorian or Julian calendar. Regardless of the date, there are similarities in celebrations. Many people will attend a holiday Mass, whether it is observed in Ukrainian or English. People will often wear traditional embroidered shirts or outfits. At the end of the Mass, the priest blesses food baskets filled with traditional paska (Easter bread), pysanky (dyed eggs), and other Easter delicacies. Accompanying the food are a holy candle and an embroidered towel. In 2020, during the COVID-19 pandemic, the Immaculate Conception Church in Hamtramck, Michigan, managed to continue this tradition by offering an online service and a drive-through blessing of Easter baskets. Many churches will also have celebratory meals where Ukrainians can get together. Traditional Easter foods include paska, pysanky, sausages, and horseradish

*Blessing Easter baskets with pysanky and paska. Immaculate Conception Church,
circa 1953.* (COURTESY OF UKRAINIAN AMERICAN ARCHIVES AND MUSEUM. CROPPED AND RECOLORED TO GRAYSCALE. USED
WITH PERMISSION.)

sauce. As a fundraiser for the parishes, communities, and Ukrainian causes,
many churches will sponsor paska sales for families that decide not to bake
it themselves.[15]

Ukrainian Schools in Michigan

There are two main types of Ukrainian schools in Michigan. The first type
is a K–12 school with an emphasis on the Ukrainian language, history, and
culture. An example is Immaculate Conception Catholic School, a parochial
school located at 29500 Westbrook Avenue, Warren, Michigan.[16] The school
belongs to the Archdiocese of Detroit Catholic Schools and offers preschool
and K–8 education for community children. Immaculate Conception has
been serving Macomb, Oakland, and Wayne counties since 1936 and is supported by the parishes of Immaculate Conception Ukrainian Catholic Church
in Hamtramck and St. Josaphat Ukrainian Catholic Church in Warren. The
school provides regular educational classes and instruction in Byzantine
Catholicism and the Ukrainian language. Even though the instruction is in
English, there is a strong emphasis on Ukrainian language and history. To

attend the school, a student does not have to be Catholic or Ukrainian, but all students receive instruction in the Catholic faith, attend Divine Liturgy (Mass), and study Ukrainian language and culture.[17] The school also provides English classes for adults who are recent immigrants to the United States and would like to improve their language skills.

The school replicates cultural practices common in Ukraine. For example, it has a special assembly at the beginning and the end of the school year called The First Bell and The Last Bell. Both assemblies are open to the public and are attended by the students and their families. At the First Bell assembly, the whole school is gathered, and one or two kindergarteners ring the bell to announce the beginning of the school year. On the last day of school, one or two graduating seniors ring the bell to finish the school year. These assemblies are very special for students, staff, and guests, and participants are often dressed in traditional embroidered clothing.

The school also has yearly assemblies to celebrate prominent Ukrainian writers like Taras Shevchenko, Lesia Ukrainka, and Ivan Franko. For the assemblies, community members hear students recite the writer's work and talk about his or her life and contribution to Ukrainian culture.[18] During the winter holidays, students have a special celebration to commemorate Saint Nickolas, who is called Sviatyi Mykolai. Saint Nickolas is the patron saint of children, and on his day well-behaved children receive presents under their pillows. Saint Nickolas Day is celebrated on December 6 according to the Gregorian calendar and December 19 according to the Julian calendar. Both are worldwide fundraising days for Ukrainian orphanages. Students perform a traditional nativity play called Vertep and a concert of carols called Koliada.[19]

Another special feature of Ukrainian American schools is their love for reciting poems and singing, practices adopted from schools in Ukraine but not typical in American K–12 education. The poems and songs are memorized by students and presented to different audiences at concerts, school board meetings, local fundraisers, and so on. Ukrainian Catholic schools pay close attention to the teaching of Ukrainian language. Students participate in all-American contests for cursive handwriting, creative writing, and the knowledge of Ukrainian culture and history.[20]

A second type of Ukrainian school in Michigan is a Saturday school called Ridna Shkola (pronounced REEHD-nah SHKOH-lah). It has an established curriculum of Ukrainian culture, history, and language. Begun in 1950 and

The Language of the Ukrainian Diaspora

Ukrainian is an East Slavic language that uses the Cyrillic alphabet. It has a complex grammar with multiple rules and exceptions, extensive vocabulary, distinctive phonological peculiarities, and a wide variety of regional and social dialects that have changed over time. This can present difficulties for second and subsequent generations of Ukrainians in the United States. Often Ukrainians of the diaspora have lexical, grammatical, and phonological features of the regional and social variety of Ukrainian spoken at the time of their immigration. Many of these features will have vanished in contemporary Ukraine, but "can still be heard occasionally in a more diluted form among descendants of some Ukrainian immigrants in the US and Canada."*

One of the unique features of the diaspora is the mixing of different regional and social dialects and blurring of their distinctions. This mixing of different dialects has often led to a blended language barely recognizable by native speakers or other Ukrainian immigrants. It would be typical for children at multiregional Plast camps to misunderstand each other even though they all were supposed to speak Ukrainian.† Nowadays, Ukrainian immigrants can learn Ukrainian online with native speakers to acquire a version of the language close to one used in Ukraine. However, many representatives of older generations of Ukrainian immigrants are not willing to update their language skills, for their language is part of their identity. Their linguistic heritage is researched by university linguists who specialize in sociolinguistics, historical linguistics, and dialectology.

* Mykola Francuzenko. "Semen Demydchuk Lecture," The Ukrainian History and Education Center, https://www.ukrhec.org/collections/archives/recorded-sound/semen-demydchuk-lecture.
† Olga Liskiwsky, personal interview, 2020.

formalized in 1952 by third-wave immigrants, the Ukrainian Educational Association's Ridna Shkola was established to educate immigrant children in language and heritage. The association's goal "was to garner financial aid from the Ukrainian community to support the Saturday school of Ukrainian studies (often called Heritage School), to ensure that the future generation would not forget its linguistic and cultural roots as they [sic] assumed their [sic] places in American society."21 A similar organization was established on Detroit's west side, but was closed in 1978. The Ridna Shkola now rents the facilities of the Immaculate Conception Ukrainian Catholic School in

Warren. The school has an eleven-year curriculum for its approximately 100 students, with final exams testing graduating proficiency in Ukrainian geography, history, culture, literature, and language.[22]

St. Mary Protectress Ukrainian Orthodox Cathedral also operates a heritage school called the Lesia Ukrainka Ukrainian Orthodox School of Language and Religion. The school opened in September 1955 with eighteen students and has had as many as 130 students from kindergarten through high school. St. Mary's notes, "This school remains an important institution in our parish and stimulates a rich cultural life and a renewal of spiritual understanding."[23] The staff and classes have been energized by recent and continuing immigration from Ukraine.

Another beneficiary of recent immigration is the University of Michigan. "U of M" has a Slavic Languages and Literatures Department, which offers courses on Russian, Polish, Czech, Ukrainian, and Balkan (Bosnian–Croatian–Serbian) cultures. Courses in Ukrainian language, literature, and culture were added in 1969 by Professor Assya Humesky, PhD. Dr. Humesky taught Ukrainian for more than twenty-five years, authored a Ukrainian grammar book, *Modern Ukrainian* (1980), and published many articles on Ukrainian language and culture.[24] Svitlana Rogovyk, Language Program Coordinator, has been teaching Ukrainian courses since 1995, designing new courses, publishing articles, and developing teaching materials. The program has grown over the years and started offering a minor in Ukrainian in 2014 along with graduate courses. The University of Michigan, according to its literature,

is the only North American University to offer a minor in Ukrainian Studies. The academic minor in Ukrainian is a multi-faceted program that integrates Ukrainian studies into broader intellectual and policy agendas while promoting research and scholarly work on contemporary Ukraine in the United States.[25]

According to Ms. Rogovyk, more than forty percent of students who minor in Ukrainian have some relation to Ukraine.[26]

Important Cultural Events

A deep and passionate interest in Ukrainian literary culture is shared in Michigan's Ukrainian American community. Many Ukrainian organizations hold regular literary readings and recitals dedicated to prominent

Ukrainian writers, poets, historical figures, composers, and others. Some of these events are held in Ukrainian only, and some in both English and Ukrainian, depending on the audience. The Detroit Ukrainian community has led efforts to promote literacy and literature, publishing "over 200 books—in genres ranging from prose, poetry, non-fiction, memoir and drama to history, politics, journalism and more" since the 1800s.[27] For example, in March 2019, the Ukrainian American Archives and Museum of Detroit held a bilingual reading of the contemporary Ukrainian poet Iryna Starovoit, whose poetry was translated and presented by Grace Mahoney, a doctoral student in the Department of Slavic Languages and Literatures at the University of Michigan.[28]

On behalf of Ukrainians in Michigan, the Ukrainian community of Detroit has worked to have the Holodomor recognized by the Michigan legislature.[29] *Holodomor* means extermination by means of starvation and refers to Stalinist Russia's genocidal famine of 1932–1933, when millions of Ukrainians were deliberately starved. Survivors of the famine and their descendants have lived in Michigan for decades. There have been multiple attempts to declare November 25 of each year as the Michigan day of remembrance of the Holodomor and to have materials on the Holodomor placed in the social studies curriculum for K–12 schools. Ukrainians from Michigan played a prominent role in opening the Holodomor memorial in Washington, DC, in 2015.[30]

Another popular cultural event is the annual Sunflower Festival. Since the 1980s, Metro-Detroit's two most active Ukrainian Catholic parishes—St. Josaphat Ukrainian Catholic Church in Warren and Immaculate Conception Ukrainian Catholic Church in Hamtramck—have collaborated to sponsor what has become one of the biggest ethnic festivals in Michigan.[31] The festival features Ukrainian foods, crafts, and dance and vocal performances. More than 25,000 visitors attend the festival, which has become a successful regional fundraiser for Ukrainian causes. The festival attracts anyone interested in Ukraine or Michigan Ukrainian American culture.

CHAPTER FIVE

Prominent Ukrainian Michiganders

As would be expected in a community valuing loyalty, patriotism, education, and hard work, many (possibly hundreds of) Ukrainian Michiganders have contributed significantly to their communities, both locally and internationally. Thirteen of these exemplary citizens deserve special recognition and are highlighted in the following sections.

Dr. Vera Andrushkiw

Born in 1942, Dr. Vera Andrushkiw was an activist, educator, and prominent member of Michigan's Ukrainian community. As a social activist, Andrushkiw led Detroit's Committee in Defense of Human Rights in Ukraine for the years 1972–1976 and advocated for the commemoration of Ukraine's Holodomor, leading seminars in Lansing and at Hope College in Holland, Michigan. She worked on creating educational curricula concerning the Holodomor for the public schools. Her humanitarian work also received high praise. When the Russian Federation invaded the Donbas, she led the Detroit Regional Council of the UNWLA and coordinated donations to soldiers and people displaced by the conflict.

During the 1970s and 1980s, she was a teacher of Ukrainian language, literature, and culture at Immaculate Conception Ukrainian Catholic High

School in Hamtramck. She also lectured in Ukrainian language and literature at Wayne State University from 1985 to 1999. In 1997–1999, she was the director of the Harvard Ukrainian Summer Institute, where she taught Advanced Ukrainian for Business. In 1985–1999, she taught Ukrainian language and literature at the University of Michigan in Ann Arbor, and in 1999–2007, she directed the Community Partnerships Program at the U.S.-Ukraine Foundation in Washington, DC.[1]

After Ukraine was granted its independence in 1991, Andrushkiw was actively involved in the development of business education in Ukraine. From 1991–1999, she organized and coordinated internships between the Lviv Institute of Management and Wayne State's School of Business. In addition, she received a grant from the U.S. Information Agency for faculty exchanges between Lviv State University, Lviv Polytechnic University, Lviv Institute of Management, and Wayne State University.

Andrushkiw was honored by Volodymyr Yelchenko, Ukrainian ambassador, "for personal contribution in strengthening a positive image of Ukraine, the development of Ukrainian education, promoting the preservation of Ukrainian cultural and historical heritage in the territory of the United States, and many years of active public work."[2] The Very Rev. Volodymyr Petriv, the dean of the Detroit Parishes, praised her "for many years of dedication, diligence[,] and valuable contributions to the Parish Communities of the Ukrainian Catholic Church of the Detroit Deanery, Michigan."[3] In 2020, Andrushkiw was given an honorary doctorate from the Ukrainian Catholic University of Lviv.[4] She passed away on March 18, 2022.

Dr. Mary V. Beck

Marusia Voitovych-Beck was a child of first-wave immigrants from the Lemko region of Western Ukraine. Beck was "born in Ford City, Pennsylvania, in 1908 to parents from Lemkivschyna, Ukraine[,] who immigrated to the United States in 1895."[5] A frequent traveler to Ukraine, Beck was a high school student in Kolomiya, Ukraine, and a member of Plast Kurin from 1921 to 1925. During the 1930s, Beck became an active member of the Ukrainian National Women's League of America and began a distinguished career in Pittsburgh as a journalist. She was editor and publisher of *Zhinochyi Svit*

(Women's World), a Ukrainian women's monthly magazine, and was the English editor for *Ukrainska Zoria* (Ukrainian Star) in Detroit and *Vilnoe Slovo* (Free Word) in Toronto. She earned her college degrees from the University of Pittsburgh (BA, 1929, LLB, 1932, converted to a JD, 1968) before moving to Detroit in 1934, where she became a social worker with Wayne County's juvenile court. She completed her credentials by passing the Michigan Bar in 1944, becoming a practicing attorney in 1947.

In 1949 Beck was the first woman to be elected to the Detroit City Council, on which she served for twenty years. She was its first female president pro tem before serving her own term from 1957 to 1961. She was Detroit's acting mayor from 1958 to 1962. Beck is known for her policies enhancing ordinary citizens' living conditions, ensuring safe drinking water, enacting historical preservation, helping the poor, supporting youth sports, preventing juvenile crime, and championing ethnic arts and culture. Beck was a political conservative and a strong advocate for national minorities. She served on the board of supervisors for nineteen years and was a supporter of the board's first African American female. Her one election bid for mayor of Detroit ended in a third-place primary defeat, as she had to split the white, law-and-order vote with moderate Roman S. Gribbs, a suburban, Polish American, former prosecutor and sheriff. In 1969 Gribbs defeated Richard Austin in the mayoral race.[6] Beck retired from politics in 1970.

The Detroit Historical Society best summarizes her work on behalf of Ukraine and Ukrainian Americans:

> Beck was deeply involved in the Ukrainian community in diaspora. Her work involved bringing attention to the horrible treatment of Ukraine and other captive states of the Soviet Union. For her work in this regard she was awarded the St. Volodymyr Medal for lifetime achievement in 2003 by the Ukrainian World Congress. She was also a patron of the arts and sponsored artists and writers who were members of the Ukrainian diaspora. Beck would go on to found the Ukrainian Women's Literary Award in Ukrainian literature as well as serve as an officer of the Ukrainian National Women's League of America (UNWLA) for the Detroit branch. Throughout her career she was a prominent speaker, with her speaking tours taking her across the United States and abroad.[7]

Much honored and well-remembered, Dr. Mary V. Beck was inducted into the Michigan Women's Hall of Fame in 1991. In 2005, at age 96, she passed away in Clinton Township.

David Bonior

David E. Bonior was born on June 6, 1945. The grandson of Polish and first-wave Ukrainian immigrants, he grew up in Hamtramck, Michigan, and attended a Latin Rite Catholic parish. He writes that "Central in my development was my religious and athletic training. . . . Combined, sports and religion instilled discipline and meaning into my young life."[8] He graduated from Notre Dame High School in Pontiac, Michigan, in 1963 and attended the University of Iowa on an athletic scholarship, graduating with a BA in 1967. In 1972, he went on to earn an MA from Chapman College in Orange, California.[9]

Bonior served in the United States Air Force during the Vietnam conflict era (1968–1972), before beginning his progressive political career. From 1973–1977, he served as a member of the Michigan House of Representatives. In 1977 he was elected to serve as a Democrat in the Ninety-fifth Congress of the United States in Washington, DC, and went on to serve through the next twelve succeeding Congresses. He served the twelfth district from 1977 to 1993 and the tenth from 1993 to 2003.[10] His legislative initiatives always advanced liberal-progressivism and touched many of its areas of concern, including labor relations, the environment, veterans' benefits and rights, wildlife preservation, students' support and rights, and, on behalf of his Ukrainian American community, honoring the victims of the Holodomor famine–genocide.[11] After government work, he became a professor, union activist, government advisor, author, and restauranteur.

Bohdan Fedorak

A third-wave immigrant, Bohdan Fedorak was born on May 7, 1933, in Kulach-kivtsi village in Western Ukraine. In 1945 his family fled to a displaced person camp in Salzburg, Austria.[12] In 1949 he immigrated to the United States, settled in Detroit, and ultimately attended Wayne State University where he earned a degree in management. He served in the U.S. military and enjoyed a successful career in the automobile industry and as an independent businessman.

Fedorak was a conservative and nationalist. He was also an active member of OUN-B (Stefan Bandera's Ukrainian Liberation Army) and served as the head of the Ukrainian National Government, which was the executive branch of the independent state proclaimed by Bandera in Lviv in 1941. In 1981 Fedorak was one of the organizers of the worldwide celebration of the fortieth anniversary of the 1941 proclamation. As a part of these festivities in Detroit, Fedorak was the head of the Business Committee and worked hard to make the celebration in Detroit memorable for the Ukrainian community of Detroit and southeast Michigan. Yaroslav Stetsko, author of Bandera's proclamation and a nationalist collaborator and wartime comrade of Bandera, was an honorary guest of the celebration.

To understand Fedorak's devotion to Bandera and the proclamation, which was considered sacred, one must understand that the document, long suppressed in the USSR, is proof that an independent Ukraine existed (at least on paper) not only in 1918 and after the collapse of the USSR in 1991, but also in 1941. The point of supporting the 1941 proclamation is to correct history. Russians have always maintained that Ukraine was *not* invaded and conquered by Soviet soldiers in 1939 or 1944, but was liberated, from Poland in 1939 and from Nazi Germany in 1944. If one recognizes the 1941 proclamation for what it claims to be, a declaration of independence, one can consider Ukraine, like all the nations overrun by the USSR and Germany, to have been independent with a "free" government-in-exile. In this light, the OUN-B and UPA partisan war (which lasted into the early 1950s) was not merely an insurrection, as claimed by the USSR, but a principled struggle to reestablish the lawful Ukrainian government. Banderites felt that there was always an orthodox and nationalistic Ukraine in which to believe and for which to fight. Fedorak's community also declared June 30, the date of Bandera's proclamation, to be the true Ukrainian Independence Day. After Stetsko's passing in 1986, Fedorak (who delivered Stetsko's eulogy) rose to replace him as head of the ABN, the Anti-Bolshevik Bloc of Nations, which included ultra-right, nationalist delegations from Ukraine, Lithuania, Latvia, Belarus, Estonia, and Hungary.[13]

Fedorak was an active member of and fundraiser for the Republican Party and organized rallies for presidents Richard Nixon, Ronald Reagan, George H. W. Bush, and George W. Bush. Fedorak was also Ukraine's Honorary Consul in Detroit from 2001 until his death in 2021. He was an active member of many Ukrainian organizations in the United States, organized conferences focused on Ukrainian issues, lobbied on behalf of the Ukrainian diaspora for any legislation designed to benefit Ukraine, and participated in many fundraising events to commemorate the Holodomor and Soviet repressions.[14] As reported in *World Today News*, "he was a public figure, president of the Regional Executive Committee of the Ukrainian Congress Committee of America, president of the Ukrainian Cultural Center [in] 'Warren' . . . Michigan, and vice president of the Ukrainian-American Freedom Foundation."[15] He passed away on May 29, 2021.

John Hodiak

Actor John Hodiak was born on April 16, 1914, in Pittsburgh to a Polish mother and Ukrainian father. The family of six (Hodiak was the eldest child) moved to Hamtramck, Michigan, where he became an outstanding athlete, singer, and actor.[16] He played baseball, sang in the parish choir, and acted in ethnic-based (Hungarian and Polish) school plays. Although he was of mixed ethnic heritage and grew up in a mixed ethnic neighborhood, he was most proud of his Ukrainian heritage and name. He is quoted as saying, "There are many reasons why I want to arrive [succeed]. I want other Ukranians [*sic*] to feel that they have a chance. Maybe not in this field, but in any other. I receive a lot of mail from Ukranians [*sic*] who thank me because I haven't changed my own name and because I don't pretend to be either Polish or Russian."[17] He passed on an opportunity with the St. Louis Cardinal farm system to continue acting. As is noted on his Hollywood star blurb,

> He first tried radio as the door to an acting career but was turned down because of his accent. He conquered the diction hurdle, became a radio actor and moved to Chicago.
>
> Two years later, after a short stint in the Army's Special Services, he arrived in Hollywood with an MGM contract.[18]

High blood pressure kept him home during World War II. But with Hollywood losing so much box office talent to the war, Hodiak made a quick rise to prominent roles, Hollywood life, and a starlet wife (Anne Baxter). After walk-on and small roles in *A Stranger in Town* (1943) and *Swing Shift Maisie* (1943), he became a leading man in *Maisie Goes to Reno* (1944). Critical approval came when he starred as Lana Turner's soldier-husband in *Marriage Is a Private Affair* (1944). Alfred Hitchcock cast him as Kovac, a victim of the U-boat war in *Lifeboat* (1944), now considered a classic. Two of his best films followed, namely, *Sunday Dinner for a Soldier* (1944) and *A Bell for Adano* (1945), "both of which showed off his quiet but rugged charm."[19]

As popular and bankable talent returned after the war, Hodiak began once again to struggle for leading roles at MGM. However, he did make notable appearances in the film noir classic *Somewhere in the Night* (1946) and in the World War II drama *Homecoming* (1948) "that starred Clark Gable and Lana Turner, with John [Hodiak] and wife Anne Baxter serving as second leads."[20] Hodiak stayed busy even as his star faded, working on both stage and screen, often in low-budget offerings, managing to be in eighteen films even as he lost box office appeal. Baxter and he divorced, yet their union produced one daughter, Katrina, who herself has acted, directed, and managed a theater company.[21] Hodiak was mounting a career comeback with *Trial* (1955) and *On the Threshold of Space* (1956) when he suffered a heart attack and died at the age of forty-one.[22]

Assya Humesky

Born in 1925 in Kharkiv, Ukraine, Dr. Assya Humesky, a third-wave immigrant, is an educator, writer, and academic administrator. She is the daughter of the famous memoirist and socialist émigré Tetyana Kardynalovska. Humesky earned her BA in French from Albertus Magnus College (1950), her MA in Slavic languages and literatures from Radcliffe College (1951), and her PhD in Slavic languages and literatures from Radcliffe–Harvard University (1955).[23] She joined the University of Michigan in 1953. There she was the advisor of the Ukrainian Students' Club and, in the 1970s, designed the university's curriculum in Ukrainian culture, literature, and language. According to the university, she

> taught all levels of Russian and Ukrainian, Russian Poetry, Russian Drama, Russian Historical Novel, Russian Stylistics, Soviet Poetry, Soviet Drama, Soviet Literature, Pushkin, Majakovsky, Chekhov, Ornamental Prose, Autobiographical Writing, Methodólogy, Ukrainian Baroque, Ukrainian Culture, Ukrainian Literature of the 1920s, Modern Ukrainian Literature, and Ukrainian Literature of the eighteenth and nineteenth centuries.[24]

During her long career she published many books and articles, her most famous being *Modern Ukrainian* (1980). In 1998 she retired as emerita professor and since has maintained a vigorous and accomplished academic life, in her own words,

> writing papers, attending conferences, doing editorial work, etc. I belong to several Ukrainian scholarly organizations: Shevchenko Scientific Society, where I head the Philological Section; The Ukrainian Academy of Arts and Sciences in the US, where I chair a similar section as well as serve as the First Vice President; and the Ukrainian American Association of University Professors, where I am also the First Vice President. We meet several times a year for conferences and discussions. I also have the duty of a copy editor for the Ukrainian Academy's yearly newsletter, not to mention editorial work on such Academy publications as the commemorative edition "Vetukhiv, the First President of the Academy" and the monograph about my sister who is now a member of the Academy "Mirtala—Sculptor and Poet." I am also on the editorial board of the magazine "Ukrajins'kyj istoryk" and the Ukrainian women's magazine "Our Life."[25]

She lives in Ann Arbor, where she continues to make contributions to Michigan's Ukrainian culture.

Edward Kozak

Cartoonist, caricaturist, and writer, Edward Kozak was born January 26, 1902, in Hirne, Stryi region, Galicia.[26] As a teenager, he served in the Ukrainian Sich riflemen in World War I (1919) and, during Ukraine's first modern independence (1917-1920), in the Ukrainian Galician army. He studied at Lviv's famed O. Novakivsky's art school from 1927-1930 and worked in Lviv's satirical and humor magazine industry—*Cross-Eyed* (1927-1933), *Mosquito* (1933-1939), and *Our Little Bell* (1932-1939)—even while producing hundreds of works as an illustrator in the then mainstream serial press for the Ukrainian Library, Library for Youth, and Large History of Ukraine. He also illustrated scores of publisher I. Tyktor's newspapers, calendars, and annuals (1933-1939).

Kozak joined the Association of Independent Ukrainian Artists in 1932 and participated in many of its exhibitions.[27] In 1939 he moved to Krakow and joined the avant-garde group "Outburst," and then returned to Lviv in

1941 at the time of the German invasion and Stefan Bandera's failed second modern independence. Kozak and his family left Ukraine for Germany in 1944 as the Soviets reconquered Ukraine, and in the displaced person camps, Kozak joined the Ukrainian Association of Artists, which he administered from 1947–1948. During this time, he also began publishing *Fox*, his own satirical magazine. After joining the third wave of Ukrainian immigration to Detroit in 1949, the magazine became *The Sly Fox*.[28]

In Detroit Kozak worked as an artist's animator in television. For his work in the educational films *Explore* and *Experience Our Past*, "he received the first prize award from the National Educational Association."[29] Still, he is best known for *The Sly Fox*, published in Detroit from 1951 to 1990, for which he was the principal writer, editor, and illustrator. Kozak participated in many group and one-man art exhibits in Ukraine, Europe, and the United States.

As an artist of over 700 paintings, EKO, as Kozak was affectionately known, worked in different and mixed media.[30] Lubow Wolnetz writes that

> thematically, his paintings were devoted to the following: the bygone life and traditions in a Ukrainian village; the lore and life of the Hutsuls;[31] heroic exploits of Ukrainian men and women in the struggle for Ukrainian independence; illustrations for Ukrainian folk songs; folk sayings and superstitions; satirical caricatures of political and civic activities in the Ukrainian community; good-natured, humorous caricatures of Ukrainian social activists, writers, artists; etc.[32]

Kozak is known for his excellence and fair-minded tone and wit. His "caricature portraits of various individuals, though satirical, are not malicious or spiteful, but are presented affectionately with warm-hearted humor."[33] According to a collector of his works, "Kozak was . . . considered the founder of Ukrainian comics."[34] In 1992, the year before his death, Kozak returned to an independent Ukraine.

John (Ivan) Panchuk

John Panchuk and his family were immigrants to two countries, first Canada and then the United States, settling in the Detroit area in 1916.[35] Born April 4, 1904, in Gardenton, Manitoba, to a first-wave Ukrainian family, Panchuk moved to Detroit and graduated from its public schools. As already noted in chapter three, Panchuk earned his BA from the University of Michigan in 1926 and his law degree from the University of Michigan in 1928. In 1929 he became a U.S. citizen.

Panchuk became a successful attorney. He began his private practice in 1929, but by 1937 he had been named state attorney general. In 1941 he took an executive position with the Federal Life and Casualty Company, managing its legal department. By 1950 "he was named secretary of the board of directors. He moved to Battle Creek in 1953 after the company moved its offices. At the time of his retirement in 1969, he had held the position of secretary and general counsel."[36]

Panchuk, however, is best remembered as the champion of third-wave immigration. As the aftermath of World War II emerged, "Panchuk was appointed by Governor G. Mennen Williams to head the state commission for displaced persons and refugees," on which he served from 1949 to 1960.[37] Even more important, he directed the United Ukrainian American Relief Committee (UUARC). His work was nothing less than heroic:

> Ukrainians relied heavily on the support of the UUARC. By 1952, the committee would help bring roughly 33,000 Ukrainian DPs [displaced persons] to the US and another 50,000 Ukrainian DPs to Canada, Australia, and several South American countries. Once the DPs arrived in the US, local UUARC committees worked to find housing for them and connected them to the local Ukrainian American community.[38]

Panchuk found sponsors and homes for thousands of third-wave immigrants. About to be resettled in Michigan, one of these immigrants, Larissa Prychodko, wrote to him of her sincere gratitude: "We are very glad to go to [the] US and we know we are indebted to you for this opportunity."[39] Like so many of Michigan's Ukrainians, the Prychodkos at first depended upon their ethnic Ukrainian community for survival, even while they connected beyond it to assimilate and advance the family:

> The Michigan chapter of the UUARC, for example, found the Prychodko family housing in Hamtramck, Michigan—the center of the Ukrainian American community in the Detroit area . . . Larissa became an adjunct faculty member in Slavic Studies at Wayne State University (WSU), where her husband became a professor in Biology. They became prominent

members of the Ukrainian community in Michigan, organizing funding for the Slavic department at WSU and giving talks about Ukrainian culture at the University of Michigan.[40]

Perhaps the highlight of Panchuk's service to Michigan, his ethnic community, and the UUARC was his 1949 immigration sponsorship of the entire Ukrainian Bandurist Chorus.[41] As with the Prychodko family, just mentioned, he and his staff facilitated the resettling of the chorus in Detroit, a process that involved finding both housing and employment for its many members.

Panchuk also presided over the Ukrainian Youth League of North America, the Ukrainian Federation of Michigan, and the Ukrainian American War Relief Committee. He maintained a lifelong passion for Eastern European studies and all things Ukrainian. He penned many articles and speeches and composed and published his family's genealogy. His best-known work was *Schevchenko's Testament*, an overview of the life, accomplishments, and influence of Ukraine's national poet. He was instrumental in the efforts to raise statues to Shevchenko in Winnepeg, Manitoba, and Washington, DC.

Politically, Panchuk was a Democrat, supporting Michigan's Democratic Party as well as directing Calhoun County's efforts to elect John F. Kennedy. His reward was the honor to serve as a Kennedy delegate at the 1960 Democratic National Convention.

Panchuk passed away on November 5, 1981.

Helen Petrauskas

Helen Petrauskas was the Ford Motor Company's first female executive and then-youngest vice-president. She worked for Ford for thirty years, primarily as vice-president of environmental and safety engineering.[42] Petrauskas was born Olena Slywynskyj in Lviv, Ukraine, in a politically active and educated family. In 1944 the Slywynskyj family escaped in a horse-drawn wagon with the three-day-old Helen just hours ahead of the advancing Soviet army.[43] They resettled as displaced persons in Austria. Sponsored by Detroit Councilwoman Mary Beck, the Slywynskyj family then joined the third wave of immigrant Ukrainians in Detroit. Assimilation was difficult, as often was the case for highly educated third-wavers. Her father Osyp Slywynskyj was an attorney in Lviv but had to settle for a machine-shop job in Detroit. Her mother Maria Slywynksyj was chronically ill with a heart condition.[44]

Helen recalled of her parents that

> They made the most of what life gave them, and retained a remarkable enthusiasm for life . . . It also taught me that a person is defined by more than what he or she does for a living. Even as a machine shop worker, my father retained a rich intellectual life. I've always appreciated the lessons my parents taught me, and tried to emulate them.

Because Petrauskas spoke Ukrainian at home and in Detroit's Ukrainian community, she entered the Detroit public school system with very little English. She remembered that she "excelled in math . . . because it was the one subject I could understand."[45] Helen was later given the opportunity to attend Cass Tech High School and then Wayne State University, graduating from Wayne in 1966 with a degree in mathematics.[46]

At Wayne State, Helen involved herself in international student activities and met Ray Petrauskas, her future husband. She recalled that "Ray had an immigrant background, too. He was Lithuanian." She noted, "What drew me to him was his boundless curiosity. He wasn't afraid to try things. He'd take anything apart to see how it worked, then put it back together." Ray, a law student, and Helen were married in 1969.[47]

Helen Petrauskas was hired by the Sherwin-Williams company as a chemist developing environmentally friendly automotive coatings. She went on to earn a law degree from Wayne State in 1971, hoping to work in antitrust litigation. Instead, she "rose quickly as the auto industry sought to cope with ever stricter anti-pollution and safety regulations. In 1983, Petrauskas became a [Ford Motor Company] vice president."[48]

She is remembered both for who she was and for what she accomplished. Coworkers described her as a

> rare person who can raise sensitive issues without raising voices. Helen wins people over with precise facts and irrefutable logic, and with a warmth that's both non-confrontational and compelling . . . Petrauskas has been convincing. She has convinced government that new environmental technologies should be phased in to best serve the public . . . convinced Ford to lead the industry in airbag implementation . . . and convinced Eastern Bloc countries on the best way to establish environmentally benign legislation.[49]

Serving on many boards both in her industry and community, she retired from Ford in 2001. She passed away from cancer in 2006.

Solomia Soroka

Violinist Solomia Soroka was born in Lviv, Ukraine, in 1971. At age ten, she made her debut as a solo artist, playing the Mendelssohn Violin Concerto with the Lviv Philharmonic Orchestra, and has since performed with other orchestras in Ukraine, Australia, and the United States.[50] She has appeared both as a soloist and as a chamber musician "at concerts and festivals in Australia, New Zealand, Germany, France, Italy, Czech Republic, Ukraine, USA, Canada, China, Korea, and Taiwan."[51] Soroka has also performed premieres of a number of important contemporary Ukrainian compositions for violin, "including works by Borys Lyatoshynsky, Myroslav Skoryk and Yevhen Stankovytch."[52] She debuted in the United States in 1997 and has since performed nationally at many major venues. An Ann Arbor resident, she frequently tours and records with her husband, the American pianist Arthur Greene. She is a violin professor at Goshen College, Indiana, and has made many recordings of prominent Ukrainian composers: Mykola Lysenko, the aforementioned Yevhen Stankovych and Myroslav Skoryk, and others. Ms. Soroka's recordings are well known in both the United States and Ukraine.[53]

Myroslava Stefaniuk

Myroslava Stefaniuk is a community activist, educator, writer, and translator.[54] She was an infant when her family fled the Soviet occupation of Ukraine after World War II. Her early childhood years were spent in a displaced persons camp in Europe until the family joined the Ukrainian third wave of immigration and resettled in the Detroit area. Stefaniuk earned a BA in English and MA in geography from Wayne State University. She went on to serve as an adjunct faculty member in geography at Wayne State. She also taught Ukrainian language and literature at Immaculate Conception Parochial Schools in Warren, Michigan.

Stefaniuk is a freelance journalist. She has penned more than 100 feature articles on art, artists, and creativity in *Ukrainian Weekly*, a national English-language weekly newspaper published in New Jersey. She also writes for Warren's *Ukrainian Metro News*, as well as numerous other periodicals. Stefaniuk contributed both poetry and prose to *At the Edge of Mirror Lake*, an anthology of Michigan authors.

Stefaniuk's books include *Dibrova Diary*, a memoir of the Ukrainian community's summer place in Brighton, Michigan, shared by five generations of

Solomia Soroka (COURTESY OF SOLOMIA SOROKA. CROPPED AND RECOLORED TO GRAYSCALE. USED WITH PERMISSION.)

Michigan Ukrainians. She and Fred Dohrs also wrote *Ukrainians of Detroit* for Wayne State University Press. This small volume in yellow and blue (Ukraine's national colors) is a respected contribution to Michigan histori- cal writing and ethnic studies and surveys the development of the Ukrainian community in Detroit.

Stefaniuk is also a valued translator of contemporary Ukrainian writing. Her translations include *Icarus with Butterfly Wings* by Vasyl Holoborodko, poetry; *Wild Dog Rose Moon* by Mykola Vorobyov, poetry; and *Parts of an Hourglass*, poetry from the gulag by Mykola Horbal. She has contributed translations to *The White Chalk of Days*, a contemporary Ukrainian literature anthology; *The Holodomor Reader*, a source book of the famine, 1932, 1933; *A Hundred Years of Youth*, a bilingual anthology of twentieth century Ukrai- nian poetry; *From Three Worlds*, contemporary writing from Ukraine; and *Shifting Borders*, Eastern European poetry of the 1980s. Stefaniuk currently lives and writes in Warren, Michigan.

Ulana Suprun

Ulana Suprun, MD, is perhaps the Michigander most important to contem- porary Ukraine. She served as acting Minister of Health of Ukraine from 2016 until 2019. Dr. Suprun's reforms have saved the lives of tens of thousands of Ukrainian soldiers and citizens and improved the lives of millions more.[55]

A daughter of third-wave Ukrainian immigrants Zenowia and George Jurkiw, Suprun was born in Detroit in 1963. She is also the granddaughter of "Maria Voloshchuk [who] participated in the Ukrainian liberation move- ment of 1930–1940."[56] Dr. Suprun attended Immaculate Conception Ukrai- nian Catholic School in Warren and graduated from Wayne State University in 1985 with a BS in biology. She went on to study medicine at Michigan State University and received her MD from this institution in 1989. "After six years of post-graduate clinical residency and fellowship . . . she was Board certified in Radiology and practiced medicine in New York, NY[,] and Detroit, MI[,] for 15 years, both in private practice and as acting director of Mammography at Henry Ford Hospital."[57] Appointments as Assistant Clinical Professor of Pathology at Mount Sinai Hospital and Vice Medical Director of Women's Imaging at Medical Imaging of Manhattan followed.[58]

Dr. Suprun has always been active in the Ukrainian diaspora community. She made her first trip to Ukraine in 1974 and followed up that visit with many more for personal and professional reasons.[59] In 2013 she and her husband Marko Suprun moved to Ukraine permanently. Dr. Suprun and Marko "were on Maidan during the Revolution of Dignity in Kyiv: Ulana worked in the medical services of the Euromaidan, while Marko helped rescue injured individuals, as well as translated for foreign journalists."[60] This experience led to the founding of Patriot Defence, which is

> a non-governmental organization that provides tactical medicine training and distributes NATO Standard Improved First Aid Kits (IFAKs) to Ukraine's servicemen . . . Dr. Suprun was instrumental in organizing several millions of dollars of humanitarian aid for Ukraine, including introducing courses in tactical medicine for over 30,000 Ukrainian soldiers and providing more than 22,000 first aid kits for those trained. The training programs also included first responder courses for police and trauma courses for both military and civilian doctors.[61]

Dr. Suprun also worked with Canadians in Ukraine who were active in humanitarian and training efforts. She was involved, for example, in the planning and implementation of the Canadian surgical missions through the Canada–Ukraine Foundation. Patriot Defence worked closely with the Canadian Embassy in Ukraine in providing training programs for Ukrainian police and first aid kits to the Ukrainian military.[62]

The Supruns were granted Ukrainian citizenship in 2015 by then president Petro Poroshenko. In September of that year, Dr. Suprun was appointed director of the School of Rehabilitation Medicine at the Ukrainian Catholic University in Lviv. Dr. Suprun also

> was invited to be a consultant for the Ukrainian Parliamentary Committee on Health and worked on new laws regarding Rehabilitation and Emergency Medicine. Through her efforts, two new professions—physical and occupational therapist—were . . . [brought to] Ukraine and academic programs . . . [devoted to the] training of these specialists were approved by the Ministry of Education.[63]

On July 27, 2016, President Petro Poroshenko's Cabinet of Ministers approved a resolution appointing Ulana Suprun, MD, as the acting Minister of Health of Ukraine. Dr. Suprun would go on to become the longest serving Minister of Health in independent Ukraine's history, holding her office until August 30, 2019. She assumed responsibility for a system that was still influenced, she wrote, by "Soviet health care . . . [and] decades of neglect, corruption and bureaucratic inefficiency."[64] She went on to say that in one hundred days, she had established a

> new team at the ministry . . . [consisting] of medical professionals who are committed to raising health care standards to European levels, to fulfill the hopes of Ukrainians who protested against a return to Soviet-style repression. Treatment entails reversing the harm done by the corruption of former President Viktor Yanukovych's regime and the legacy of the Soviet Union.[65]

Dr. Suprun's reforms are transformational and broad-based. Administrative practices and structures were updated and streamlined. A single-payer health care insurance system was designed and implemented. Medical professional compensation was increased, and medicine for the chronically ill was subsidized. A strong push against bribery and other forms of corruption was made.[66] In 2019 a new government came to power in Ukraine, and Dr. Suprun, as is customary with a change of administrations, was replaced, whereupon she returned to her medical and nongovernmental organization work in Lviv.

Stefan Tymoshenko

While he spent less than a decade in Michigan, Stefan Tymoshenko, considered the "father of applied mechanics," is one of Michigan's most influential Ukrainian immigrants.[67] He was born in Shepetivka, Ukraine, on December 23, 1878. He was educated in St. Petersburg, Russia, where he also served as an instructor. Appointments in Kyiv and Zagreb followed. Joining the second wave of Ukrainian immigrants in 1922, he came to Pittsburgh, Pennsylvania, to join the engineering staff of Westinghouse Electric and Manufacturing Company.[68] In 1927 he moved to Michigan and joined the faculty of the University of Michigan in Ann Arbor. In the next nine years, he finished his education, adding a PhD in electrical engineering to his already impressive credentials, and chaired the Theoretical Mechanics Department. As noted by Paul Chenea, Timoshenko

offered courses in Advanced Strength of Materials, Elasticity, Elastic Stability, Thin Plates and Shells, Vibration Analysis, Advanced Dynamics,
Plasticity, and other advanced topics. Graduate students came from all
over the world to study under Timoshenko and then to return to spread his
fame. At Michigan he continued to draw famous colleagues, and the Summer Symposia of the Engineering Mechanics Department became known
worldwide for their distinguished lectures. His students of this era became
the foremost teachers of mechanics . . . today, and many of them are now
the guiding heads of large research organizations.[69]

Timoshenko published seven books while in Ann Arbor. In 1936 he transferred his Michigan academic success to Stanford University, from which
he retired in 1944 and at which he was granted emeritus status.[70] In all, Timoshenko authored thirteen textbooks. His first, published in Russia in 1911,
was entitled *Strength of Materials*, and was translated into more than ten
languages.[71] "So great was his influence," it is written, "that his active years in
the field became known as 'the Timoshenko era.'"[72] He passed away in 1972.

Conclusion

As a developing nation, the United States depended upon and profited much from its immigrants, among them approximately one million Ukrainians. Following network lines, four separate waves of Ukrainians took advantage of the opportunity structures across North America, settling and prospering on prairie farms, in the mines of Eastern coal fields, and in the factories, retail stores, and offices of New York, Chicago, Cleveland, Milwaukee, and Detroit. Called to Michigan by the need for cheap, adaptable, and hard-working laborers, Ukrainians have thrived in Michigan's mining, forest, agricultural, manufacturing, and intellectual communities. Since the late nineteenth century, Michigan's Ukrainians are noteworthy for their intense commitment to the following:

- *Ukrainian Catholic and Orthodox parishes and schools*, fostering the development of knowledge, the arts, intellectuality, spirituality, language learning, and a timeless cultural heritage;
- *Ukrainian history, culture, and literature*, sponsoring musical groups, literary gatherings, publishing ventures, and exhibits of national uniqueness and pride; and
- *the old country and families left behind*, raising awareness of political and social difficulties in Ukraine, donating money to Ukrainian

charities and institutions, and supporting new immigrant groups fleeing political, economic, and religious persecution.

While Ukrainians now emigrate to Michigan in much lower numbers, they are still coming. New immigrants are likely to be much different from their parents, grandparents, and great-grandparents, however, and may not be as noticeable. There has always been an interesting tension in America's immigrant stories between individual ethnic uniqueness, standing out, and assimilation, blending in. Both tendencies can be admired for their benefits, and both can be expressed. Because Ukrainians look like Western and Northern Europeans, historically America's favored immigrants, Ukrainians with advanced English abilities, pronounceable names, and marketable skills have almost always been successful in building an American life. Nativistic prejudices against eastern Europeans generally have faded—at least for a time. Names are anglicized, marriages across different ethnic and religious groups are made, vernacular English is mastered, and accents are diminished. After all, Ukrainians are savvy consumers of our contemporary Western culture.

To stand out or blend in, or, as Robert D. Putnam might ask, to bond or bridge? One of the striking and determining characteristics of Michigan's contemporary Ukrainian immigrants is the ability to choose to what extent they will practice Ukrainian traditions and culture in the United States. There are immigrants who come to Michigan and immediately join the Ukrainian community. They might have known about Michigan while still living in Ukraine and have come through social networks to the state. They attend Michigan's Ukrainian orthodox churches, try to find jobs in Ukrainian-speaking companies, send their children to Ridna Shkola weekend schools and Plast summer camps, speak Ukrainian at home, support their old-country families, and try to visit their homeland as often as possible. These people use social media to organize their social life within Michigan's Ukrainian community, whether it be in Warren, Detroit, Flint, Traverse City, or any number of Detroit suburbs or Michigan small towns. There are multiple pages on different social media dedicated to Michigan's Ukrainians. These pages have advertisements in Ukrainian or English (sometimes both languages) for employment opportunities, private Ukrainian day care centers, garage sales, catering businesses, and cultural events. Often, people in

The Hamtramck Disneyland

Third-wave immigrant Dmytro Szylak came to the United States from Lviv in 1949 and worked as an assembly-line worker at the General Motors factory in Hamtramck. After he retired, he created a sculpture on and over the roofs of his two houses. The installation became an iconic representation of Szylak's third-wave immigrant experience and his love of Ukraine and the United States. The installation has references to the local mayor, the American flag, U.S. and Ukrainian maps, the Ukrainian Insurgent Army, the Ukrainian flag and its colors, and Ukrainian history, in particular Ukraine's independence from Russia. Locals call it "The Hamtramck Disneyland," and it has become an important part of Hamtramck culture, helping to make the city one of the most diverse in Michigan. After Szylak's death in 2015, the installation was maintained by locals, few of whom were Ukrainian. The Hamtramck-based nonprofit art collective "Hatch Art" now owns the installation and has made it a home to four artist residencies and an art gallery, keeping alive the legacy of Szylak and the Ukrainian community in Hamtramck, which can be dated from the late nineteenth century and Ukrainian first-wave immigrants.*

* David Lewinsky, in Liana Aghajanian, "The Disneyland of Detroit. How an Art Installation Created by a Ukrainian-American Auto-plant Worker Has Become a Symbol for the Hope and Heartbreak of Immigrants." *Pacific Standard*, December 18, 2017.

this group bond and forge strong relationships within Michigan's Ukrainian community and organize their lives ethnically. They also use their talents and skills to promote themselves within the Ukrainian community and often use their ethnicity to advance themselves. For example, Olga Liskiwsky became the executive director of the Ukrainian Museum and Archive after retiring from her mainstream accounting job. Violinist Solomia Soroka, now an American academician, organized an exhibit of her father's work at this same museum.

On the other hand, there are a significant number of Ukrainians who might not even know about the existence of the Ukrainian community in Michigan, who speak English at home to master English language skills as soon as possible, visit Ukraine only rarely, and try to separate themselves

Mykola Liskiwsky, circa 1946 (COURTESY OF UKRAINIAN AMERICAN ARCHIVES AND MUSEUM. CROPPED AND RECOLORED TO GRAYSCALE. USED WITH PERMISSION.)

from Ukrainian society while maintaining minimal (but acceptable) social connections with family and friends left behind—all without bonding within Michigan's Ukrainian community.

Michigan children of Ukrainian immigrants also make a choice about how much of their Ukrainian identity to recognize and practice. They can fall in love with Ukrainian music, crafts, and traditions and try to maintain them in their adult lives. They can take Ukrainian as a foreign language at the University of Michigan, travel to Ukraine, and even work in Ukraine or for Ukrainian American companies in the United States—or not. Only the hero's journey, after all, requires a return to the homeland. As was mentioned, "getting ahead," an American guiding principle, requires "bridging" outside the ethnic group.

Michigan's Ukrainian immigration story is the triumph of a vibrant nationality called to freedom, opportunity, safety, prosperity, and the hero's journey. In the following closing vignette, Olga Liskiwsky dramatizes the Ukrainian immigrants' profound commitment to their homeland, Ukraine's tragic past, and family members left behind.[1] She recounts her father's heroic return to his homeland to find and visit his family's graves. Mykola Liskiwsky, a member of the famed Ukrainian Bandurist Chorus and the son of a Ukrainian priest, was a third-wave Ukrainian immigrant to Michigan. Like many in this post-World War II group, he and his wife came from the displaced persons camps in Europe. This remembrance is a postscript to the study you've just read.

The Hero's Return

Olga Liskiwsky

My ninety-seven-year-old father Mykola asked me to join him on a trip to his native homeland in Central Ukraine. The purpose of the visit was to locate the graves of his father, mother, and grandmother. My father lost his mother Olha when he was two years old. Mykola's father, Fr. Ivan, had been arrested and shot by a Soviet NKVD execution squad (the NKVD was the USSR's People's Commissariat for Internal Affairs) in the mid-1920s. His body was given to his then teenaged son Mykola to bury. The boy had a carpenter build a simple coffin and then lined it with his own drawings since he had nothing else.

Previously, both my siblings and my mother traveled to his village of Mykhailivtsi in the Vinnytsia Oblast (Central Ukraine) over the last couple of years trying to locate these unmarked graves, but had not succeeded. And so, in July 2007, my father and I journeyed to Ukraine. It had been nearly eighty years since my father had been to his village. After his father's murder, he had lived in the village for a time, but when he was alerted to the danger he would face because he was the son of a priest, he fled to Zhmerynka and much later ended up in Kyiv. There he attended the Kyiv Conservatory of Music and became a member of the Ukrainian Bandurist Chorus (1941).

Our first stop was Kyiv to visit St. Sophia Cathedral, my father's fervent and long-standing wish. Rather than going directly inside the church, my father went over to one of the rounded outer walls. His hands shook as he touched the whitewashed, plastered brick, crying that he had thought he would never see or touch them again. Afterward, we made our way to the newly reconstructed St. Michael's Golden Domed Monastery across the wide street. Concerned with my father's growing fatigue and the impending rain, I asked him to wait within the archway of the complex while I exchanged currency so that we might take a taxi back to our family's apartment. When I returned, my father had a smile on his face. After I left, he had taken off his hat, as was fitting on the grounds of this holy site. He was standing, leaning on his cane and looking around, when he noticed that a young boy, thinking that my father was one of the elderly beggars who often stand outside churches in Ukraine asking for alms (mylostynia), was throwing coins into his hat. My father further astonished his small benefactor when he tried to return the coins to him.

The next day we began our journey to my father's home village. We traveled southwest from Kyiv to Andrusivka, where we stopped for the evening. Our journey ran through Berdychiv, Vinnytsia, Zhmerynka, and then finally to Mykhailivtsi. Upon arriving, we stopped first at the refurbished village Church of the Nativity of the Theotokos, where my grandfather Fr. Ivan served until his arrest and execution. I had the honor of watching as my father entered this Church, where he himself had prayed, sang, and directed the youth choir. Our guide was the head of the village council, Leonid Barhatiuk, who took us to the cemetery, telling us that this area was the last possible place someone could have been buried. Upon arriving, my father shook his head and said that this was not the place. The area where his father was buried was near the old sacristan's house. Leonid said, there was no such house. My father asked, "Are you originally from this village?" Barhatiuk said he was not.

My father directed us to where the sacristan's house had stood. He took his cane and tapped around the ground until he found the original foundation. My father got his bearings and turning west to the area of great overgrown trees and bushes, he said, "Through there is a clearing where an old chapel stood. I buried my father near my mother and grandmother's graves there."

Nearby, two young children and their father lived. They joined our exploration, telling us, "Yes, there are many stone crosses toppled over" in that area. They pulled me along through the dense overgrowth saying, "We can't read the dates on the gravestones, they are in Church Slavonic, so come, we'll show you." We crawled through the bushes and suddenly the area opened to a clearing with a large metal cross. The children ran ahead and when I caught up with them, I saw the stone crosses they had described to me. My father, too, had entered the clearing, but by then, he was confused since the chapel was not where he remembered it. The children's father comforted us by saying that his grandmother had told him that there had been an old chapel just where my father remembered, but it had been torn down in the 1930s.

Leonid took me aside and said, "Let's take your father to my house to rest, and I'll have some men from the village clear this area. Then we can have a better look."

We went to Leonid's home, where he and his family made us feel welcome. My father could not sleep for a long time, and he sat up remembering stories about the village—the ancient burial mounds of the Kozaks, the life of the parish Church and parochial school, and how in the 1920s the Soviets had confiscated the church bell and other items. He shared these memories with Leonid, who by then was sitting at my father's feet learning about the tragic history of his village. The next day, after the men had cleared the trees, we were back at the cemetery. To our astonishment, many graves covered in green myrtle had been revealed. We located a grouping of three mounds of earth, the graves of my father's family. My father's dream had been realized.

After his lonely and lifesaving flight from this village, he endured many hardships, including imprisonment, slave labor, the upheavals and losses of World War II, displaced persons camps, and immigration with the rest of the Bandurist Chorus to an unknown land called "Michigan." While he and his wife Olena established a family and new life in Detroit, they never forgot their homeland. Mykola had been reluctant to return home while it was still part of the Soviet Union. With this trip, however, after Ukrainian independence and near the end of his life, he was finally able to return to his childhood village and the graves of his family. His journey had closed the circle with his past. My mother traveled to Ukraine a few days later to join him. Together they ordered a commemorative plaque with the names of his family and placed it near the three newly discovered graves.

Ford Motor Company Tables

NATIONALITY	NUMBER OF EMPLOYEES	NUMBER OF EMPLOYEES IN GOOD NEIGHBORHOODS	NUMBER OF EMPLOYEES IN FAIR NEIGHBORHOODS	NUMBER OF EMPLOYEES IN POOR NEIGHBORHOODS
American	16,457	15,208	1,243	6
Polish	7,525	6,646	835	44
Italian	1,954	1,578	360	16
Canadian	1,819	1,718	100	1
Roumanian	1,750	1,417	303	30
Jewish*	1,437	1,243	190	4
German	1,360	1,229	130	1
Russian	1,160	1,055	104	1
English	1,159	1,071	88	0
Hungarian	690	600	88	2
Austrian	573	525	46	2
Syrian	555	471	74	10
Lithuanian	541	490	49	2
Scotch	480	447	33	0
Serbian	456	398	54	4
Armenian	437	417	20	0
Irish	399	380	19	0
Ruthenian	368	320	47	1
Greek	281	247	33	1
Bohemian	240	222	18	0
TOTAL	40,903	36,840	3,933	130

Table 4. Neighborhood Conditions of Employees, according to Nationality, as of January 12, 1917

SOURCE: FORD MOTOR COMPANY, "STATISTICAL ANALYSES OF WORKERS' HOMES AND HABITS [MY TITLE]," THE HENRY FORD MUSEUM ARCHIVES, DEARBORN, MI, JUNE 16, 2019.

* FORD'S MOTIVATION FOR THIS CATEGORY REFLECTS THE BELIEF AT THE TIME THAT JEWISH ETHNIC DISTINCTION WAS EQUATED WITH NATIONALITY. THIS "SINGLING OUT" OF AN ETHNIC GROUP REFLECTS A COMMON (AT THE TIME) FORM OF ANTISEMITISM. IN 1917, THE JEWISH STATE OF ISRAEL DID NOT YET EXIST. SEE PBS, *AMERICAN EXPERIENCE*, "FORD'S ANTI-SEMITISM," HTTPS://WWW.PBS.ORG/WGBH/AMERICANEXPERIENCE/FEATURES/HENRYFORD-ANTISEMITISM/.

Table 5. Acknowledged Habits of Employees, according to Nationality, as of January 12, 1917				
NATIONALITY	**NUMBER OF EMPLOYEES**	**NUMBER OF EMPLOYEES OF GOOD HABITS**	**NUMBER OF EMPLOYEES OF FAIR HABITS**	**NUMBER OF EMPLOYEES OF POOR HABITS**
American	16,457	13,981	2,428	48
Polish	7,525	5,078	2,417	30
Italian	1,954	1,406	535	13
Canadian	1,819	1,635	183	1
Roumanian	1,750	1,197	552	1
Jewish*	1,437	1,291	143	3
German	1,360	1,073	284	3
Russian	1,160	842	315	3
English	1,159	1,076	82	1
Hungarian	690	499	189	2
Austrian	573	445	123	5
Syrian	555	476	77	2
Lithuanian	541	390	149	2
Scotch	480	443	36	1
Serbian	456	330	124	2
Armenian	437	437	381	55
Irish	399	343	56	0
Ruthenian	368	244	124	0
Greek	281	210	71	0
Bohemian	240	184	56	0
TOTAL	40,903	32,622	8,163	118

SOURCE: FORD MOTOR COMPANY, "STATISTICAL ANALYSES OF WORKERS' HOMES AND HABITS [MY TITLE]," THE HENRY FORD MUSEUM ARCHIVES, DEARBORN, MI, JUNE 16, 2019.

* FORD'S MOTIVATION FOR THIS CATEGORY REFLECTS THE BELIEF AT THE TIME THAT JEWISH ETHNIC DISTINCTION WAS EQUATED WITH NATIONALITY. THIS "SINGLING OUT" OF AN ETHNIC GROUP REFLECTS A COMMON (AT THE TIME) FORM OF ANTISEMITISM. IN 1917, THE JEWISH STATE OF ISRAEL DID NOT YET EXIST. SEE PBS, AMERICAN EXPERIENCE, "FORD'S ANTI-SEMITISM," HTTPS://WWW.PBS.ORG/WGBH/AMERICANEXPERIENCE/FEATURES/HENRYFORD-ANTISEMITISM/.

NATIONALITY	NUMBER OF EMPLOYEES	NUMBER OF EMPLOYEES WITH GOOD HOME CONDITIONS	NUMBER OF EMPLOYEES WITH FAIR HOME CONDITIONS	NUMBER OF EMPLOYEES WITH POOR HOME CONDITIONS
American	16,457	15,159	1,256	42
Polish	7,525	6,211	1,181	133
Italian	1,954	1,478	412	64
Canadian	1,819	1,772	41	6
Roumanian	1,750	1,325	331	94
Jewish*	1,437	1,306	124	7
German	1,360	1,254	101	5
Russian	1,160	978	157	25
English	1,159	1,115	39	5
Hungarian	690	572	102	16
Austrian	573	497	65	11
Syrian	555	423	100	32
Lithuanian	541	477	55	9
Scotch	480	467	13	0
Serbian	456	386	53	17
Armenian	437	424	11	2
Irish	399	381	18	0
Ruthenian	368	273	86	9
Greek	281	241	38	2
Bohemian	240	202	34	4
TOTAL	40,903	36,111	4,297	495

Table 6. Living Conditions of Employees, according to Nationality, as of January 12, 1917

SOURCE: FORD MOTOR COMPANY, "STATISTICAL ANALYSES OF WORKERS' HOMES AND HABITS [MY TITLE]," THE HENRY FORD MUSEUM ARCHIVES, DEARBORN, MI, JUNE 16, 2019.

* FORD'S MOTIVATION FOR THIS CATEGORY REFLECTS THE BELIEF AT THE TIME THAT JEWISH ETHNIC DISTINCTION WAS EQUATED WITH NATIONALITY. THIS "SINGLING OUT" OF AN ETHNIC GROUP REFLECTS A COMMON (AT THE TIME) FORM OF ANTISEMITISM. IN 1917, THE JEWISH STATE OF ISRAEL DID NOT YET EXIST. SEE PBS, AMERICAN EXPERIENCE, "FORD'S ANTI-SEMITISM," HTTPS://WWW.PBS.ORG/WGBH/AMERICANEXPERIENCE/FEATURES/HENRYFORD-ANTISEMITISM/.

Notes

Introduction

1. John Panchuk. "First Ukrainians in Detroit," in Michael Wichorek and Martha Wichorek, Ukrainians in Detroit (Detroit: privately printed, 1968), 9.

2. There is a competing version of this narrative with a Mychailo Stefanksy as the principal character who "arrived in Detroit with his wife and eight children to settle on Canfield Street. He obtained work with Weber Lumber and soon was building houses in the Michigan-Livernois area." Petro Rohatysnkyj, "History of Ukrainian Settlement in the Metropolitan Detroit Area," *Ukrainians in Detroit and Michigan: Commemorating the Millennium of Christianity in Ukraine* (Detroit: Ukrainian Millennium Council, 1988), 465.

3. The hero's journey is an idea echoed in Stephanie A. Bohon and Meghan Conley, *Immigration and Population* (Cambridge, UK: Polity Press, 2015), 2. The hero's journey, as theorized by Joseph Campbell and others, is a quest narrative in which a singular character is called to adventure, travels beyond the world of his or her guardians, is tempted and tried by adversity, overcomes setbacks, is transformed and blessed, and returns to the land (or state of being) from which he or she set forth originally. Scott Jeffrey, "How to Use the Hero's Journey for Storytelling and Personal Transformation," CEO Sage, https://scottjeffrey.com/heros-journey.

4. Emma Lazarus, "The New Colossus," Poetry Foundation, https://www.

poetryfoundation.org/poems/46550/the-new-colossus.

5. Myron B. Kuropas, "Ukrainians and Ukrainian Americans, 1870–1940," in *Immigrants in American History: Arrival, Adaptation, and Integration*, vol. 2, ed. Elliott Robert Barkan (Santa Barbara, CA: ABC-CLIO, 2013), 649.

6. Ibid., 649. According to Vladimir Werstman, "Ukrainians were known and recorded in the past under different names: Rusyns, Ruthenians, Rusniaks, and Little Russians, as well as under regional names such as Carpatho-Russians, Boykos, Hutsuls, Galitzians, Bukovinians." Vladimir Werstman, *The Ukrainians in America, 1608–1975: A Chronology and Fact Book* (Dobbs Ferry, NY: Oceana, 1976), iv. Hutsuls, Boykos, and Lemkos are ethnic subgroups of Ruthenians with their own dialects and social customs.

7. For example, Olivier Zunz makes no specific or detailed discussion of Ukrainians in Detroit in his otherwise excellent *The Changing Face of Inequality* (see Sources and Further References). For him, Ukrainians are rolled either into other Central or Eastern European groups or into the category of Russian Jews.

8. David A. Gerber, *American Immigration: A Very Short Introduction* (New York: Oxford University Press, 2011), 3.

Chapter One. The Old Country

1. Matt Soniak, "Why Did 'The Ukraine' Become Just 'Ukraine'?," *Mental Floss*, January 12, 2013.

2. Ibid.

3. Orest Subtelny, *Ukrainians in North America* (Toronto: University of Toronto Press, 1991), 13.

4. Ibid.

5. Immigrants, write Bohon and Conley, follow "network lines shaped by cultural, geographic, and historical conditions." That means immigration patterns are not a haphazard rush of people bent on appropriating others' wealth. Immigration patterns show a systematic search for and assimilation into complex opportunity structures. Bohon and Conley, 2.

6. Subtelny, 13.

7. Ibid., 4, 6.

8. There was no modern banking system. The Jewish minority controlled commerce in the cities and taverns in the villages, the two sources of local money lending. Moreover, interest rates were from 150 to 250 percent annually. Ibid., 8–9.

9. Ibid., 8.

10. Paul M. Hedeen, "Maryna Hedeen," personal interview, July 6, 2020.

11. Myroslava Stefaniuk and Fred E. Dohrs, *Ukrainians of Detroit* (Detroit: Wayne State University, 1979), 47–48.

12. Lemkos were an ethnic subgroup of Ruthenians from Western Ukraine. Galicia is a region of Western Ukraine. "Galicians" might include Jews, Poles, or any of the ethnic Ruthenian subgroups from the region like Hutsuls, Lemkos, and Boykos.

13. Waslyl Halich, *Ukrainians in the United States* (New York: Arno Press, 1970), 28.

14. Ibid., 29.

15. Ibid.

16. Ibid.

17. Ibid., 30–31.

18. Ibid., 30.

19. Subtelny, 20.

20. Ibid., 17.

21. Ibid., 19.

22. Shirley Blumenthal, *Coming to America: Immigrants from Eastern Europe* (New York: Delacorte Press, 1981), 98.

23. Osyp Krawczeniuk, Dr., *The Ukrainian Church in America: Its Beginnings* (Detroit: Ukrainian Millennium Committee of Detroit, 1988), 3.

24. Subtelny, 29.

25. Ibid.

26. Ibid.

27. Halich, 35.

28. Ibid.

29. Ibid., 32.

30. Ibid., 33.

31. Nancy Karen Wichar, *Ukrainians of Metropolitan Detroit* (Chicago: Arcadia, 2009), 7.

32. Ashley Johnson Bavery, *Bootlegged Aliens: Immigration Politics on America's Northern Border* (Philadelphia: University of Pennsylvania Press, 2020), 14.

33. Ibid.

34. Ibid., 26.

35. Then and now, this is the story of many U.S. immigrant and minority groups. It is important to note that the greater the *visual* difference from Anglo-Saxon and Scandinavian immigrants, the slower and more protracted is the immigrant's

struggle for equal access to opportunity structures.

36. David M. Brownstone and Irene Franck, *Facts About American Immigration* (Bronx, NY: H. W. Wilson Co., 2001), 727–34.

37. Bavery, 13.

38. Brownstone and Franck, 727–34.

39. Bavery, 14.

40. Ibid.

41. Stefaniuk and Dohrs, 45.

42. Subtelny, 102.

43. Bavery, 12–13. "Ghost walkers" refers to the illegal immigrants' practice of winter crossings of the Detroit river over the ice while wearing white bedsheets or plasterers' suits for camouflage.

44. Subtelny, 28.

45. Ibid.

46. Ibid.

47. Ibid., 105.

48. *Holodomor: Ukrainian Genocide in the Early 1930s* (Kyiv: Ukrainian Institute of National Memory, no date), 4.

49. Ibid.

50. Myron Kuropas, *Ukrainians in America* (Minneapolis: Lerner, 1972), 33.

51. Robert Conquest, *The Great Terror: A Reassessment* (Oxford: Oxford University Press, 2008), 227–34. Brandon Lewis, "Preface," *The Crime of Moscow in Vynnytsia* (Torrance, CA: Institute for Historical Review, 1951), 5. "The Hero's Return," Olga Liskiwsky's remembrance concluding *Ukrainians in Michigan*, is occasioned by the murder of her paternal grandfather in The Great Terror.

52. Kuropas, *Ukrainians in America*, 27, 33.

53. Subtelny, 104.

54. Brownstone and Franck, 283–84; Subtelny, 104.

55. Subtelny, 109. This nationalism shared features with nationalistic movements in Germany, Spain, Italy, Romania, and Poland. All were anathema to the Soviet Union.

56. Ibid.

57. Ibid., 112.

58. Ibid., 113.

59. This date has also been cited as 1948–1970. Kuropas, "Ukrainians and Ukrainian Americans, 1870–1940," 649.

60. "Molotov-Ribbentrop: Five States Remember 'Misery' Pact Victims," *BBC News*, August 23, 2019.

61. Maria Savchyn Pyskir, *Thousands of Roads: A Memoir of a Young Woman's Life in the Ukrainian Underground During and After World War II*, trans. Ania Savage (Jefferson, NC: McFarland, 2001), 15.

62. Ibid., 16.

63. "Molotov-Ribbentrop."

64. Pyskir, 20.

65. Christopher R. Browning, *Ordinary Men: Reserve Police Battalion 101 and the Final Solution in Poland* (New York: Harper Perennial, 1998), 18.

66. Timothy Snyder, *Bloodlands: Europe Between Hitler and Stalin* (New York, Basic Books, 2010), ix–x.

67. Snyder, vii–viii.

68. After the Germans were finally expelled in late 1944, rival nationalistic and communistic partisan armies (OUN and UPA) as well as Soviet troops maintained active hostilities in Western and Central Ukraine until the 1950s. Pyskir, 129.

69. Kuropas, *Ukrainians in America*, 36.

70. Brownstone and Franck, 731.

71. Ibid., 734.

72. Ibid.

73. Kuropas, *Ukrainians in America*, 39.

74. Jaroslava Maria Petrykevich, *A Study of the Development of Ukrainian Organizations in Metropolitan Detroit* (MA thesis, Wayne State University, Detroit, 1971), 29. Among the refugees there were OUN nationalists, UPA fighters, and former Nazi collaborators, some of whom had been involved in the persecution of Jews. How many will never be known.

75. Kuropas, "Ukrainians and Ukrainian Americans, 1870–1940," 649.

76. UAPOST.US, "The History of Ukrainian Immigration to the US," Ukrainian-American Media, entry posted May 5, 2019, http://www.uapost.us/en/blog/the-history-of-ukrainian-immigration-to-the-us.

77. For exceptions, see Chapter Three's discussion of Ukrainian communities beyond Metro-Detroit and notes regarding the Traverse City community of immigrants fleeing religious persecution and the Russian Federation's invasion of Crimea and the Donbas.

Chapter Two. Ukrainians in Detroit

1. Frank B. Woodford and Arthur M. Woodford, *All Our Yesterdays: A Brief History of Detroit* (Detroit: Wayne State University Press, 1969), 35–41.

2. Ibid., 42.

3. Ibid., 49.

4. Ibid., 73–74.

5. Ibid., 106–25, 134.

6. Ibid., 143.

7. Ibid., 138.

8. Olivier Zunz, *The Changing Face of Inequality: Urbanization, Industrial Development, and Immigrants in Detroit, 1880–1920* (Chicago: University of Chicago Press, 1982), 3.

9. Ibid.

10. Ibid., 26.

11. Ibid., 16.

12. Ibid., 19.

13. Woodford and Woodford, 369.

14. Ibid.

15. Ibid.

16. Ibid.

17. Ibid.

18. Detroit Historical Society, "Industrial Detroit (1860–1900)," https://detroithistorical.org/learn/timeline-detroit/industrial-detroit-1860–1900.

19. Woodford and Woodford, 370.

20. Ibid.

21. Ibid.

22. Detroit Historical Society.

23. Ibid.

24. Detroit: A Planning History, "Detroit 1900–1930," https://detroitplanninghistory.weebly.com/1900–1930.html.

25. Ibid.

26. Titled respectively "Neighborhood," "Habits," "Home Conditions," these analyses were reflective of Ford's insistence that his immigrant workers have adequate housing and live clean, productive lives. Ford employed sociologists to visit Ford-furnished housing and to report on workers' home lives. Such analyses seem intrusive and paternalistic now. However, we must remember the

crush of first- and second-wave immigration and the lack of adequate housing in Detroit. Given nativistic suspicions directed toward orthodox immigrants, the tumultuous situations of the Detroit automotive boom, World War I, and the collapse of the great empires of Europe, these analyses seem more apt. They allowed Ford to know, shape, control, and Americanize the immigrants in his work force. Ford Motor Company, "Statistical Analyses of Workers' Homes and Habits [my title]" (Henry Ford Museum Archives, Dearborn, MI), 2019. See the Appendix for abridged tables.

27. Werstman, iv.

28. Robert A. Rockaway, *The Jews of Detroit: From the Beginning, 1762–1914* (Detroit: Wayne State University Press, 1986), 52.

29. Ibid.

30. Wichorek and Wichorek, 9.

31. Stefaniuk and Dohrs, 84.

32. Andrew M. Greeley, *Why Can't They Be Like Us* (New York: Institute of Human Relations Press, American Jewish Committee, 1969), 31–32.

33. Petrykevich, 16.

34. Ibid., 17.

35. Stefaniuk and Dohrs, 78.

36. Wichorek and Wichorek, 9.

37. Petro Rohatynskyj, "History of Ukrainian Settlement in the Metropolitan Detroit Area," *Ukrainians in Detroit and Michigan: Commemorating the Millennium of Christianity in Ukraine* (Detroit: Ukrainian Millennium Council, 1988), 465.

38. Ibid.

39. Stefaniuk and Dohrs, 79.

40. This parish consecrated a new church in 1948. It is still at Gilbert and Clayton Streets and is now called Saints Peter and Paul Orthodox Christian Cathedral. It considers itself a missionary church without any national (other than American) identification. "About Us," Saints Peter & Paul Orthodox Christian Cathedral, https://www.ssppdetroit.org.

41. Zunz, 5.

42. Ibid.

43. Rohatynskyj, 465. The original frame structure and the Ukrainian Home were torn down in 1967. The modern Immaculate Conception Church at Commor and McDougall had been welcoming parishioners since 1942. See also Wichorek and Wichorek, 11.

44. Sebastian Sabol, Metropolitan Detroit Ukrainian Millennium Council, "Ukrainian Churches and Religious Organizations," *Ukrainians in Detroit and Michigan: Commemorating the Millennium of Christianity in Ukraine* (Detroit: Ukrainian Millennium Council, 1988), 487–509. Unless otherwise noted, parish histories are from this source.

45. "Our History," St. Michael the Archangel Parish, http://stmichaelarchangel. org/?page_id=23.

46. Elizabeth Symonenko, "October 11, 2014," Facebook, https://www.facebook. com/search/top?q=Ukrainian%20orthodox%20church%20of%20the%20holy%20 trinity%20in%20dearborn%20mi.

47. Rohatynskyj, 466.

48. Petrykevich, 18.

49. Halich, 76–77.

50. Petrykevich, 45–46.

51. Rohatynskyj, 467–68; Ukrainian American Archives and Museum, "Ukrainian National Temple in Detroit," In Search of Our Local History Blog, entry posted June 8, 2020, https://www.ukrainianmuseumdetroit.org/blog-1?offset=1592195884236.

52. Zunz, 3.

53. Ibid., 5

54. Rockaway, 54.

55. Ibid.

56. Ibid, 55.

57. Greeley, 33; Petrykevich, 19. Zunz concurs when he recognizes this same phase as the beginning of the divisive influence of social class.

58. Ibid., 19.

59. Rohatynskyj, 468

60. Ibid.

61. Ibid.

62. Ibid.

63. Ibid.

64. Stefaniuk and Dohrs, 85.

65. Rohatynskyj, 469.

66. Ibid. Parishes were not simple places of worship. Evolving like the social strata around them, they became complex social constructions that included choirs, worship schools, academic schools (primary and secondary levels), mission

organizations, retreat and travel groups, ladies' auxiliaries, clubs for all age
groups, and altar boy groups and choirs. Various parish committees drew in not
only women, who seem to predominate in church activities and school support,
but also men from the business community.

67. While Petrykevich (following Greeley) hypothesizes a further four through six
phases for "old" or first groups of immigrants, this writer finds this analysis
overly schematic. In the case of Ukrainian immigration to Detroit and Michigan,
it was often the same people populating the rosters of aid societies, parishes,
women's groups, and political groups. Be that as it may, women took leadership
in the third phase of the first two waves of immigration as the community began
to assert itself culturally, socially, artistically, and politically. This advocacy
gained tremendous energy with the arrival of the Ukrainian third wave.

68. Rohatynskyj, 469.

69. Ibid.

70. Ibid. The selling of government bonds to finance the enormous cost of the
military began in World War I and was perfected in World War II: "Non-
negotiable Series E 'Defense Bonds' were introduced in $25, $50, and $1,000
denominations. The $25 bonds became the most publicized and most popular,
selling for $18.75 and maturing over a ten-year period to pay the bondholder $25.
Beginning in 1942, these bonds . . . could be purchased on an installment plan
through payroll deductions at the work place [sic] . . . [and] an installment plan
was even established for school children who could buy twenty-five cent war
stamps to paste into a book until they saved the $18.75 needed to buy a $25 war
bond." See National Museum of the Army, "Reflections—Wartime Bond Drives,"
https://armyhistory.org/reflections-wartime-bond-drives.

71. Stefaniuk and Dohrs, 85.

72. Ibid.

73. Rohatynskyj, 469.

74. Ibid. In 1933, these included Ivan Panchuk and Joseph Czarnowsky. The Federation
also helped launch Mary Beck's 1949 campaign for the Detroit City Council.

75. Petrykevich, 45–46.

76. Wichorek and Wichorek, 170.

77. Wayne State University Slavic Klub, "Get Involved," https://getinvolved.wayne.
edu/organization/wayne-state-university-slavic-klub.

78. The Ukrainian Graduates, "Home," http://www.ukrainiangraduates.org/history.
html.

79. Ibid.

80. Wayne State University, Department of German/Slavic Studies, "Welcome to the Ukrainian Room," http://www.clas.wayne.edu/Ukrainian_room/index.html.

81. Teresa Pickering, "Ukrainian Room, Ukrainian Club, Ukrainian Graduates," message to the author, February 11, 2020, e-mail.

82. Stefaniuk and Dohrs, 86.

83. Petrykevich, 22.

84. Ibid., 23.

85. See chapter 1, note 68 in this volume.

86. Petrykevich, 29–30.

87. Ibid.

88. At one time it was reported to Heinrich Himmler, the leader of Hitler's SS, that there were 900,000 Eastern European "volunteers" serving in the German armed forces and navy. See Chris Bishop, *Hitler's Foreign Divisions, Foreign Volunteers in the Waffen SS, 1940–1945* (London: Amber, 2005), 82. With the exception of the Ukrainian Waffen SS Division (14th Galician), most of these troops were blended with the Wehrmacht garrisons in Western Europe. Memoirs of the Normandy invasion and fighting make repeated references to Russian, Polish, and Ukrainian soldiers among the German prisoners and casualties. For example, see Holger Eckhertz, *D Day Through German Eyes: Book One and Two* (Germany: DTZ, 2016), 221. Ukrainian involvement in the Holocaust is heavily documented. One recent treatment is Wendy Lower, *The Ravine: A Family, A Photograph, A Holocaust Massacre* (Boston: Houghton Mifflin Harcourt, 2021), 31. In most cases, the level of fear and coercion influencing the "volunteering" was significant. "Trawniki" refers to a specific concentration camp where volunteers—most often Russian and Ukrainian POWs trying to avoid extermination themselves—were trained to serve at other camps like Sobibor, Belzec, and Treblinka.

89. Petrykevich., 31.

90. Ibid.

91. Ibid., 43–44.

92. Ukrainian Cultural Center (UCC), "Home," https://www.uccwarren.com/?fbclid=IwAR17ZSKEQA_aL6dmlv1zywGGj2wEvq6cHUmxuFhSYFBaT3k-Tr_qJg3l94A.

93. Ibid.

94. Discuss Detroit, "Ukrainian Worker's Home," April 6, 2006, https://www.

atdetroit.net/forum/messages/62684/69957.html.

95. Ukrainian American Archives & Museum, "History of Museum," https://www.ukrainianmuseumdetroit.org/our-museum-1.

96. Ibid., "Our Museum."

97. Myrosia Stefaniuk, *Dibrova Diary* (Saline, MI, privately printed, 2018), 5.

98. Maria Lisowsky, "Detroit Branch of Plast Celebrates its 50th Anniversary," *Ukrainian Weekly*, December 26, 1999.

99. Plast Detroit, "What Is Plast?," http://www.plastdetroit.org/what-is-plast.

100. Ibid.

101. Ibid.

102. Ukrainian Bandurist Chorus, "About Us," https://www.bandura.org/aboutus; Orest Sushko, dir., *Music of Survival: The Story of the Ukrainian Bandurist Chorus*, DVD, prod. Orest Sushko (Living Strings Productions, Inc., 2014).

103. Olena Danylyuk, "Ukrainians in Michigan," message to Maryna Hedeen, July 14, 2020, e-mail.

104. Woodford and Woodford, 343.

105. Ibid.

106. Zunz, 402.

107. Ibid.

108. Ibid., 403.

109. Robert D. Putnam, *Bowling Alone: The Collapse and Revival of American Community* (New York: Simon & Schuster, 2000), 22.

110. Ibid., 23.

111. Ibid., 22.

112. Ibid., 23.

113. Ibid., 22.

114. Ibid.

115. Ibid., 23.

116. Ibid.

117. Zunz, 403.

118. Joe T. Darden and Richard W. Thomas, *Detroit: Race Riots, Racial Conflicts, and Efforts to Bridge the Racial Divide* (East Lansing: Michigan State University Press, 2013), 137–46.

119. U.S. Census Data, "Ukrainian Americans," https://en.wikipedia.org/wiki/Ukrainian-Americans.

Chapter Three. Beyond Metro-Detroit

1. Halich, 52, 155.

2. Halich, 32; Magnaghi, 141, 151.

3. Halich, 52

4. Wasyl Ohar, "Ukrainians in Ann Arbor," in *Ukrainians in Detroit and Michigan: Commemorating the Millennium of Christianity in Ukraine* (Detroit: Ukrainian Millennium Council, 1988), 474.

5. Ibid. See Dr. Tymoshenko's brief biography in Chapter Five.

6. Ibid.

7. Ibid.

8. Ibid., 475.

9. Ibid.

10. Ibid.

11. Ibid., 476. See Dr. Humesky's brief biography in Chapter Five.

12. Ibid., 477.

13. Ibid.

14. Andrij Zakala, "Ukrainians in Jackson," in *Ukrainians in Detroit and Michigan: Commemorating the Millennium of Christianity in Ukraine* (Detroit: Ukrainian Millennium Council, 1988), 479.

15. Ibid.

16. Ibid.

17. St. Michael Ukrainian Catholic Church, "About Us," https://stmichaelgrandrapids.org/about.

18. Ibid.

19. Ibid.

20. Transfiguration Skete, "Holy Protection Monastery," https://www.societystjohn.com/magnificat.

21. Ibid.

22. Stepan Stefaniw, Wolodymyr Pytlowanyj, and Dr. Nicholas Bartkiw, "Ukrainians in Flint," in *Ukrainians in Detroit and Michigan: Commemorating the Millennium of Christianity in Ukraine* (Detroit: Ukrainian Millennium Council, 1988), 481.

23. Ibid.

24. Ibid.

25. Ibid.

26. Ibid.

27. Ibid.

28. Ibid.

29. "Ukrainians in Saginaw," in *Ukrainians in Detroit and Michigan: Commemorating the Millennium of Christianity in Ukraine* (Detroit: Ukrainian Millennium Council, 1988), 482.

30. Ibid.

31. "Ukrainians in Muskegon Heights," in *Ukrainians in Detroit and Michigan: Commemorating the Millennium of Christianity in Ukraine* (Detroit: Ukrainian Millennium Council, 1988), 483.

32. Paul M. Hedeen, "Laurence Zaremba," personal interview, June 15, 2021.

33. "Ukrainians in Muskegon Heights," 483.

34. Ibid.

35. "Thriving Local Ukrainian Community Turns Attention to Homeland," *Traverse City Record Eagle*, May 9, 2015.

36. "Faith, Family, and Freedom: Traverse City's Ukrainian Community," *Northern Express*, January 1, 2016, https://www.northernexpress.com. The Crimean invasion was undertaken under the guise of an annexation and a referendum, the Donbas under the guise of a separatist movement. Both invasions, however, were not only sponsored by the Russian Federation but carried out by its military units. Both were gross violations of international law, Ukrainian sovereignty, previous treaty arrangements, and international human rights. The February 2022 outright invasion of Ukraine is a continuation of the 2014 violations.

37. "Local Church Rallying Behind Ukrainian Pastor," *UpNorthLive*, https:// upnorthlive.com, September 9, 2014.

38. "United by Faith: Joint Pentecost Service Embraces Ukrainian, American Traditions," *Traverse City Record Eagle*, May 14, 2016.

Chapter Four. Traditional Cultural Practices of Michigan's Ukrainians

1. T. Nikolaeva, "Traditional Clothing and Its Variants," *Etnodim*, https://etnodim. com.ua/ua/ua-tsikava-informatsiya/121-tradytsiynyyodayh.

2. "Ukrainian Traditional Necklaces: From Trypillia Ceramics to Venetian Glass and Corals," *Ostannia Barykada*, http://obarykada.com/chasopys/necklaces.

3. Marta Pisetska Farley, *Festive Ukrainian Cooking* (Pittsburgh: University of Pittsburgh Press, 1990), xiv–xv.

4. Maria Prus, "What a Real Borsch Is and Peculiarities of the Cuisine of American

Diaspora. Conversation with Marianna Dushar, aka Pani Stefa," Voice of America, January 29, 2021, https://ukrainian.voanews.com/a/pani-stefa-interview/5755176.html.

5. Kateryna Mischenko, "Ukrainian Year: Holidays That Unite Us," The National Center of Folk Culture "Ivan Honchar Museum," https://honchar.org.ua/p/ukrajinskyj-rik-svyata-scho-nas-objednuyut.

6. "Today, October 14, Ukrainians celebrate the Feast of the Protection of Our Most Holy Lady ([Cover]) and the Defender of Ukraine Day ([Defenders of the Fatherland Day])," Ukrainian Institute of America, https://ukrainianinstitute.org, October 14, 2019.

7. "Christmas in Ukraine," *Christmas Around the World from World Book* (Chicago: World Book, Inc., 1997), 9.

8. Olena Stepanchenko, "The Astral Map of the World in Ukrainian Carols," The National Center of Folk Culture "Ivan Honchar Museum," https://honchar.org.ua/p/astralna-karta-svitu-v-ukrajinskyh-kolyadkah.

9. "Ivan Kupala Night: A Slavic Solstice Celebration In Ukraine," *Radio Free Europe Radio Liberty*, https://www.rferl.org/a/ivan-kupala-night-ukraine/31320288.html.

10. Dzvinka Nykorak Hayda, et al., "A Cultural Thread: The Enduring Ukrainian Spirit," Ukrainian American Archives and Museum of Detroit in Conjunction with the Detroit Historical Society (Detroit, 2013), 21, 22.

11. Olga Kari, *Fruit Punch with Pattypan Squashes* (Kyiv: Publishing House "Komora," 2020), 152.

12. "Christmas in the USA," Radio Svoboda, https://www.radiosvoboda.org/a/897907.html.

13. Kateryna Mischenko, "Ukrainian Year: Holidays That Unite Us," The National Center of Folk Culture "Ivan Honchar Museum," https://honchar.org.ua/p/ukrajinskyj-rik-svyata-scho-nas-objednuyut.

14. "Christmas in Ukraine," op. cit., 45.

15. Lyudmyla Strazhnyk, "Easter in the USA: How Ukrainians from the Frankivsk Region Celebrate Easter Abroad," *Reporter*, April 29, 2016, https://report.if.ua/kultura/velykden-v-ameryci.

16. "Immaculate Conception Ukrainian Catholic Schools," *Facebook*, https://www.facebook.com/pg/www.icschools2015/about/?ref=page_internal.

17. "Frequently Asked Questions," Immaculate Conception Catholic Schools, https://www.icschoolswarren.org/faq-s.

18. Ibid.

19. "Immaculate Conception Ukrainian Catholic Schools," Ibid.

20. Ibid.

21. Metropolitan Detroit Ukrainian Millennium Council, *Ukrainians in Detroit and Michigan: Commemorating the Millennium of Christianity in Ukraine* (Detroit: Ukrainian Millennium Council, 1988), 553.

22. "Final Exams," School of Ukrainian Language and Culture, Detroit, Michigan, http://ukrainianschooldetroit.org/%d0%bc%d0%b0%d1%82%d1%83%d1%80%d0%bo-final-exams.

23. "School of Religion and Ukrainian Studies," St. Mary the Protectress Ukrainian Orthodox Cathedral, http://protectress.org/index.php?option=com_content&view=article&id=74&Itemid=484.

24. Ruth Shamraj, "Reflections on My Love of Languages and Literatures: A Ukrainian Literary Evening with Professor Assya Humesky," *The Slavic Scene* 30 (2019). Dr. Humesky is also profiled in this book's chapter 5.

25. The University of Michigan, "Slavic Languages and Cultures," https://lsa.umich.edu/slavic/undergraduate-students/majors---minors/ukrainian.html.

26. Svitlana Rogovyk, personal interview, July 9, 2020.

27. Ksenia Rychtycka, "Program Celebrates 100 Years of Literary Publications by Michigan Ukrainians," *Ukrainian Weekly*, December 20, 2019.

28. Ksenia Rychtycka, "Ukrainian American Archives and Museum Presents Contemporary Ukrainian Poetry in Translation," *Ukrainian Weekly*, April 20, 2018, https://www.ukrweekly.com/.

29. "Rep. Howrylak Calls for Annual Ukrainian Holodomor Memorial Day in Michigan," Michigan House Republicans, http://gophouse.org/rep-howrylak-calls-annual-ukrainian-holodomor-memorial-day-michigan.

30. Doris Duzyj, "Update from Detroit Holodomor Committee," *Ukrainian Weekly*, October 26, 2018; Melissa Nann Burke, "Ukrainian Americans Honor Victims of Genocidal Famine," *The Detroit News*, November 7, 2015.

31. Carl Levin, "Ukrainian Sunflower Festival," *Local Legacies: Celebrating Community Roots*. The American Folklife Center, The Library of Congress, http://memory.loc.gov/diglib/legacies/loc.afc.afc-legacies.200003171.

Chapter Five. Prominent Ukrainian Michiganders

1. Oksana Malanchuk, "Ukrainian Cultural Center of Detroit spotlights members of UNWLA, Vera Andrushkiw receives honorary doctorate from UCU," *Ukrainian Weekly*, March 27, 2020.

2. Ibid.

3. Ibid.

4. Matthew Matuszak, "UCU Awarded Honorary Doctorate to Vera Andrushkiw," Ukrainian Catholic Educational Foundation, February 12, 2020.

5. Roman Dacko, "Biography," Printout from the *Mary Beck Collection and Archive* (Detroit: Ukrainian American Archives & Museum, 2021). All information concerning Dr. Mary V. Beck is from the Ukrainian American Archives and museum unless otherwise noted.

6. Darden and Thomas, 95.

7. "Mary V. Beck," *Encyclopedia of Detroit*, Detroit Historical Society, https://detroithistorical.org/learn/encyclopedia-of-detroit/beck-mary-v.

8. David E. Bonior, *Whip: Leading the Progressive Battle During the Rise of the Right* (Westport: City Point Press, 2018), viii.

9. Ibid.

10. "Bonior, David Edward," *History, Art and Archives, United States House of Representatives*, https://history.house.gov/People/Detail/9583.

11. "Legislation Sponsored or Cosponsored by David E. Bonior," Congress.Gov, https://www.congress.gov/member/david-bonior/B000619.

12. Stefan Romaniv, "In Memory of Our Friend Bohdan Fedorak," Nationalistic Portal, trans. Maryna Hedeen, http://ukrnationalism.com/news/nationalist-movement/4376-pamiati-druha-bohdana-fedoraka.html.

13. V. Scherbiy, "[Commemorating Fortieth Anniversary of the Act of Ukrainian Independent State in Detroit, Michigan]," *The Herald of the Organization of the Defense of the Four Freedoms of Ukraine*, trans. Maryna Hedeen, https://diasporiana.org.ua/wp-content/uploads/books/4932/file.pdf.

14. Stefan Romaniv. On behalf of the Ukrainian diaspora in Michigan and the world, Fedorak sent a significant monetary contribution for a 2005 monument to commemorate the hundreds of prominent Ukrainians who were killed in 1937–1938 in Sandarmokh, Karelia, following Stalin's order "About Anti-Soviet elements" issued on August 5, 1937.

15. "Consul of Ukraine in the USA Died," *World Today News*, May 30, 2021.

16. Gary Brumburgh, "John Hodiak, Biography," *IMDb,* https://www.imdb.com/name/nm0388303/bio.

17. Ibid.

18. "John Hodiak," *Los Angeles Times, Hollywood Star Walk*, http://projects.latimes.com/hollywood/star-walk/john-hodiak.

19. Brumburgh, ibid.

20. Ibid.

21. "Katrina Hodiak," IMDb, https://www.imdb.com/name/nm0388304/
bio?ref_=nm_ov_bio_sm#mini_bio.

22. Brumburgh, ibid.

23. "Assya Humesky," LSA, *Slavic Languages and Literatures, University of Michigan,*
https://lsa.umich.edu/slavic/people/faculty/assyakh.html.

24. Assya Humesky, "Staying Connected," *Slavic Scene,* Volume 15, Number 1, May
2007.

25. Ibid.

26. S. Hordynsky, " Edward Kozak," *Ukrainian Folklife Archive,* https://archives.
ukrfolk.ca/index.php/kozak-edward.

27. "Edward Kozak," Ukrainian Art Library, http://en.uartlib.org/ukrainian-artists/
kozak-edward.

28. Ibid.

29. Lubow Wolnetz, "A Gift of Twenty-Two Edvard Kozak Paintings," *Sower* (January
26, 2014), The Ukrainian Museum and Library of Stamford.

30. Ibid.

31. Like Lemkos and Boykos, Hutsuls are an ethnic minority subgroup of
Ruthenians occupying isolated areas of Western Ukraine. Each subgroup speaks
its own distinctive dialect as well as Ukrainian.

32. Ibid.

33. Ibid.

34. "Kozak, Edvard (EKO), 1902–1992, Collection of Satirical Magazines *Lys Mykyta,*
1947–1985 (217 issues)," *Rare Paper: Books and Ephemera,* https://www.
rare-paper.com/pages/books/152/edvard-kozak-eko/collection-of-satirical-
magazines-lys-mykyta-1947-1985-217-issues.

35. "Biography," *John Panchuk Papers: 1913–1981,* Bentley Historical Library,
University of Michigan, https://quod.lib.umich.edu/b/bhlead/umich-bhl-
85346?rgn=main;view=text. Unless otherwise noted, all information is from this
source.

36. Ibid.

37. Ibid.

38. "Letter from Larissa Prychodko to John Panchuk," John Panchuk Papers, Box 2,
Bentley Historical Library, University of Michigan, https://perspectives.ushmm.
org/item/letter-from-larissa-prychodko-to-john-panchuk.

39. Ibid.

40. Ibid.

41. The Ukrainian Bandurist Chorus is discussed in Chapter Two.

42. Patricia Sullivan, "Helen Petrauskas, 61; Ford's Top Safety Exec Promoted Air Bags," *Los Angeles Times*, March 13, 2006.

43. "Ford's Top Woman Champions Safety and Health Issues-and Does it With a Smile," *American Woman Motorscene*, https://www.theautochannel.com/mania/women/oldawm/awm09952.html.

44. Ibid.

45. Ibid.

46. Sullivan, ibid.

47. "Ford's Top Woman . . . ," ibid.

48. Ibid.

49. Ibid.

50. Solomia Soroka, "Biography," solomiasoroka.com, http://solomiasoroka.com/recordings.

51. Ibid.

52. Ibid.

53. Solomia Soroka, "Recordings," solomiasoroka.com, http://solomiasoroka.com/recordings.

54. Myroslava Stefaniuk, "Biography," Message to Paul M. Hedeen, June 22, 2021, e-mail. All information is from this source.

55. "Dr. Ulana Suprun," Wilson Center, https://www.wilsoncenter.org/person/dr-ulana-suprun.

56. "Suprun Ulana (Ulana Suprun), Biography," *TAdvisor: Government, Business, IT*, https://tadviser.com/index.php/Person:Ulana_Suprun.

57. "Dr. Ulana Suprun," ibid.

58. Ibid.

59. "Suprun Ulana . . . ," ibid.

60. "Dr. Ulana Suprun," ibid.

61. Ibid.

62. Ibid.

63. Ibid.

64. Ulana Suprun, "100 Days of Health Care Reform in Ukraine," *U.S. News and World Report*, December 22, 2016.

65. Ibid.

66. "Dr. Ulana Suprun," ibid.

67. "Stephen Timoshenko—Path-Breaking Professor of Applied Mechanics," *Stanford Engineering*, https://engineering.stanford.edu/about/heroes/2012-heroes/stephen-timoshenko.

68. "Stephen Timoshenko," American Institute of Physics: Physics History Network, https://history.aip.org/phn/11610014.html.

69. Paul Chenea, "Stephen Timoshenko, Bio," Faculty History Project, University of Michigan, http://faculty-history.dc.umich.edu/faculty/stephen-timoshenko/bio-o.

70. "Stephen Timoshenko," American Institute of Physics," op. cit.

71. "Stephen Timoshenko—Path-Breaking Professor," op. cit.

72. Ibid.

Conclusion

1. Olha Liskiwsky, "Article about the Remembrance of My Father Mykola Liskiwsky," Message to Maryna Hedeen, August 14, 2020, e-mail.

Sources and Further References

Aghajanian, Liana. "The Disneyland of Detroit. How an Art Installation Created by a Ukrainian-American Auto-Plant Worker Has Become a Symbol for the Hope and Heartbreak of Immigrants." *Pacific Standard*, December/January 2018.

Allen, W. E. *The Ukraine: A History*. Cambridge: Cambridge University Press, 1963.

Auerback, Frank L. *The Admission and Resettlement of Displaced Persons in the United States*. New York: Common Council for American Unity, 1949.

Bekh, Olena, and James Dingley. *Ukrainian*. New York: McGraw-Hill. 2003

Bilinsky, Yaroslav. *The Second Soviet Republic: Ukraine After World War II*. New Brunswick, NJ: Rutgers University Press, 1962.

Bishop, Chris. *Hitler's Foreign Divisions, Foreign Volunteers in the Waffen SS, 1940–1945*. London: Amber, 2005.

Blumenthal, Shirley. *Coming to America: Immigrants from Eastern Europe*. New York: Delacorte Press, 1981.

Bohon, Stephanie A., and Meghan Conley. *Immigration and Population*. Cambridge, UK: Polity Press, 2015.

Boileau, Lowell. "Ukrainian Worker's Home." *Detroit Yes, E-News*. https://www.detroityes.com/news/070426/601pics/201.htm.

Bonior, David E. *Whip: Leading the Progressive Battle During the Rise of the Right*. Westport, CT: City Point Press, 2018.

Borjas, George J. *We Wanted Workers: Unraveling the Immigration Narrative*. New

York: W. W. Norton and Co., 2016.

Boyd, Herb. *Black Detroit: A People's History of Self-Determination*. New York: Amistad, an imprint of Harper-Collins, 2018.

Browning, Christopher R. *Ordinary Men: Reserve Police Battalion 101 and the Final Solution in Poland*. New York: Harper, 1998.

Browning, Christopher R., and Jürgen Matthäus. *The Origins of the Final Solution: The Evolution of Nazi Jewish Policy, September 1939–March 1942*. Lincoln: University of Nebraska Press; Jerusalem: Yad Vashem, 2004.

Brownstone, David M., and Irene Franck. *Facts About American Immigration*. Bronx, NY: H. W. Wilson Co., 2001.

Burke, Melissa Nann. "Ukrainian Americans Honor Victims of Genocidal Famine." *Detroit News*, November 7, 2015.

"Christmas in Ukraine." *Christmas Around the World from World Book*. Chicago: World Book, Inc., 1997.

Conquest, Robert. *The Great Terror: A Reassessment*. Oxford: Oxford University Press, 2008.

"Consul of Ukraine in the USA Died." *World Today News*, May 30, 2021.

Cybriwsky, Roman. *Ukrainians in the USA and Canada According to Published Census Data*. New York: Ukrainian Center for Social Research, 1975.

Dacko, Roman. "Biography." Printout from the *Mary Beck Collection and Archive*. Detroit: Ukrainian American Archives & Museum, 2021.

Darden, Joe T., and Richard W. Thomas. *Detroit: Race Riots, Racial Conflicts, and Efforts to Bridge the Racial Divide*. East Lansing: Michigan State University Press, 2013.

Davidowicz, Lucy S. *The Jewish Presence*. New York: Harcourt Brace Jovanovich, 1978.

———. *The War Against the Jews, 1933–1945*. New York: Holt, Rinehart, Winston, 1975.

Des Pres, Terrence. *The Survivor*. New York: Oxford University Press, 1976.

Dzul, Paul, ed. *Ukrainians in Detroit and Michigan: Commemorating the Millennium of Christianity in Ukraine*. Detroit: Metropolitan Detroit Ukrainian Millennium Council. 1988.

Eckhertz, Holger. *D Day Through German Eyes: Book One and Two*. Germany: DTZ, 2016.

Evans, Andrew. *Ukraine*. Guilford, CT: Globe Pequot Press, 2007.

"Faith, Family, and Freedom: Traverse City's Ukrainian Community." *Northern Express*, January 1, 2016.

Farley, Marta Pisetska. *Festive Ukrainian Cooking*. Pittsburgh: University of Pittsburgh Press, 1990.

Gajecky, George. "One Thousand Years of Christianity in Ukraine." *Ukrainians in Detroit and Michigan: Commemorating the Millennium of Christianity in Ukraine*. Detroit: Metropolitan Detroit Ukrainian Millennium Council, 1988.

Gerber, David A. *American Immigration: A Very Short Introduction*. New York: Oxford University Press, 2011.

Gjelten, Tom. *A Nation of Nations: A Great American Immigration Story*. New York: Simon & Schuster, 2015.

Greeley, Andrew M. *Why Can't They Be Like Us*. New York: Institute of Human Relations Press, The American Jewish Committee, 1969.

Greene, Victor R. *The Slavic Community on Strike: Immigrant Labor in Pennsylvania Anthracite*. Notre Dame, IN: University of Notre Dame Press, 1968.

Halich, Wasyl. *Ukrainians in the United States*. New York: Arno Press, 1970.

Handlin, Oscar. *The Uprooted*. Boston: Atlantic Monthly Press, 1973.

Hayda, Dzvinka Nykorak, et al. "A Cultural Thread: The Enduring Ukrainian Spirit." Ukrainian American Archives and Museum of Detroit in Conjunction with the Detroit Historical Society. Detroit, 2013.

"History of Detroit, Michigan." *United States History*. https://www.u-s-history.com/pages/h2116.html.

Holodomor: Ukrainian Genocide in the Early 1930s. Kyiv: The Ukrainian Institute of National Memory (no date).

Hooker, Clarence. *Life in the Shadows of the Crystal Palace, 1910–1927*. Bowling Green, OH: Bowling Green University Popular Press, 1997.

Horniatkevych, Demian, and Lidiia Nenadkevych. "Embroidery." *Encyclopedia of Ukraine*, vol. 1. Toronto: University of Toronto Press, 1984.

Hrushevsky, Michael. *A History of Ukraine*. New Haven, CT: Yale University Press, 1941.

"John Hodiak." *Los Angeles Times, Hollywood Star Walk*, October 20, 1955.

Kari, Olga. *Fruit Punch with Pattypan Squashes*. Kyiv: Publishing House "Komora," 2020.

Klimchak, Maria, et al. *From DP to DC: Displaced Persons: A Story of Ukrainian Refugees in Europe, 1945–1952*. Chicago: Ukrainian National Museum of Chicago, 2011.

Koonz, Claudia. *The Nazi Conscience*. Cambridge, MA: Belknap Press, 2003.

Kostiuk, A. *Stalinist Rule in the Ukraine: A Study of the Decade of Mass Terror*. New

York: Praeger, 1977.

"Kozak, Edvard (EKO), 1902–1992, Collection of Satirical Magazines Lys Mykyta, 1947–1985 (217 issues)." *Rare Paper: Books and Ephemera.* https://www. rare-paper.com/pages/books/152/edvard-kozak-eko/collection-of-satirical-magazines-lys-mykyta-1947–1985–217-issues.

Krawczeniuk, Osyp. *The Ukrainian Church in America: Its Beginnings.* Detroit: Ukrainian Millennium Committee of Detroit, 1988.

Kuropas, Myron B. *Ukrainians in America.* Minneapolis: Lerner, 1972.

———. "Ukrainians and Ukrainian Americans, 1870–1940." In *Immigrants in American History: Arrival, Adaptation, and Integration,* vol. 2. Ed. Elliott Robert Barkan. Santa Barbara, CA: ABC-CLIO, 2013.

"Leontovych, Mykola." *Internet Encyclopedia of Ukraine.* http://www. encyclopediaofukraine.com/display.asp?linkpath=pages%5CL%5CE%5CLeonto vychMykola.html.

Lewis, Brandon. "Preface." *The Crime of Moscow in Vynnytsia.* Torrance, CA: Institute for Historical Review, 1951.

Liebenson, Maureen Mostyn. *Christmas in Ukraine.* Chicago: World Book, Inc., 1997.

Lisowsky, Maria. "Detroit Branch of Plast Celebrates its 50th Anniversary." *Ukrainian Weekly.* http://www.ukrweekly.com/.

Lower, Wendy. *The Ravine: A Family, A Photograph, A Holocaust Massacre.* Boston: Houghton Mifflin Harcourt, 2021.

Magnaghi, Russell M. *Upper Peninsula of Michigan: A History.* Morrisville, NC: Lulu Press, 2017.

Malanchuk, Oksana. "Ukrainian Cultural Center of Detroit spotlights members of UNWLA, Vera Andrushkiw receives honorary doctorate from UCU." *Ukrainian Weekly.* March 27, 2020.

Matuszak, Matthew. "UCU Awarded Honorary Doctorate to Vera Andrushkiw." Ukrainian Catholic Educational Foundation, February 12, 2020.

Metropolitan Detroit Ukrainian Millennium Council. "Ukrainian Churches and Religious Organizations." *Ukrainians in Detroit and Michigan: Commemorating the Millennium of Christianity in Ukraine.* Detroit: Ukrainian Millennium Council, 1988.

"Molotov-Ribbentrop: Five States Remember 'Misery' Pact Victims." *BBC News,* August 23, 2019.

"Mother of God in Icons and Old Prints." The National Center of Folk Culture "Ivan Honchar Museum." https://honchar.org.ua/events/bohorodytsya-v-narodnij-ikoni-ta-starodrukah.

Nakonechny, Jim, Rev. "Ask a Priest." *Ukrainian Catholic Eparchy of Edmonton.*
http://eeparchy.com/2020/09/08what-is-the-difference-between-the-ukrainian-catholic-church-and-ukrainian-orthodox-church-and-the-roman-catholic-church.

"The Nazi Occupation of Soviet Ukraine." *Encyclopedia Brittanica.* brittanica.com.

Ohar, Wasyl. "Ukrainians in Ann Arbor." *Ukrainians in Detroit and Michigan: Commemorating the Millennium of Christianity in Ukraine.* Detroit: Ukrainian Millennium Council, 1988.

"Orthodox Organization Sponsors Christmas Concert in Southfield." *Morning Sun.* https://www.themorningsun.com/lifestyles/orthodox-organization-sponsors-christmas-concert-in-southfield/article_8a3d0d68-0927-5f1e-a7b4-98b3896dc7b1.html.

Panchuk, John. "First Ukrainians in Detroit." In Michael Wichorek and Martha Wichorek, *Ukrainians in Detroit.* Detroit: privately printed, 1968.

Petrykevich, Jaroslava Maria. "A Study of the Development of Ukrainian Organizations in Metropolitan Detroit." MA thesis, Wayne State University, Detroit, 1971.

Prchal, Tim, and Tony Trigilio, eds., *Visions and Divisions: American Immigration Literature, 1870–1930.* New Brunswick, NJ: Rutgers University Press, 2008.

Prus, Maria. "What a Real Borsch Is and Peculiarities of the Cuisine of American Diaspora: Conversation with Marianna Dushar, aka Pani Stefa." *Voice of America,* January 29, 2021.

Putnam, Robert D. *Bowling Alone: The Collapse and Revival of American Community.* New York: Simon & Schuster, 2000.

"Pysanky from the Chernihiv Region." Ukrainian American Archives & Museum. May 11, 2020.

Pyskir, Maria Savchyn. *Thousands of Roads: A Memoir of a Young Woman's Life in the Ukrainian Underground During and After World War II.* Translated by Ania Savage. Jefferson, NC: McFarland, 2001.

Randall, Francis B. *Stalin's Russia.* New York: Free Press, 1965.

Rockaway, Robert A. *The Jews of Detroit: From the Beginning, 1762–1914.* Detroit: Wayne State University Press, 1986.

Rohatynskyj, Petro. "History of Ukrainian Settlement in the Metropolitan Detroit Area." In *Ukrainians in Detroit and Michigan: Commemorating the Millennium of Christianity in Ukraine.* Detroit: Ukrainian Millennium Council, 1988.

Rychtycka, Ksenia. "Michigan History Conference Spotlights Local Ukrainian Community." *Ukrainian Weekly*, March 24, 2017.

Sabol, Sebastian. "Ukrainian Churches and Religious Organizations." In *Ukrainians in Detroit and Michigan: Commemorating the Millennium of Christianity in Ukraine*. Detroit: Ukrainian Millennium Council, 1988.

Sands, Phillippe. *East West Street*. New York: Vintage, 2017.

Satenstein, Liana. "Ukraine's Influence on the Runway Is Bigger Than You Think." *Vogue*, February 1, 2017.

Seniuk, Roman. "Pysanky by Roman Seniuk." http://romanseniuk.tripod.com.

Shamraj, Ruth. "Reflections on My Love of Languages and Literatures: A Ukrainian Literary Evening with Professor Assya Humesky." *The Slavic Scene* 30 (2019).

Snyder, Timothy. *Bloodlands: Europe Between Hitler and Stalin*. New York: Basic, 2010.

Soniak, Matt. "Why Did 'The Ukraine' Become Just 'Ukraine'?" *Mental Floss*, January 12, 2013.

"Statistical Analyses of Workers' Homes and Habits" [authors' title]. Ford Motor Company. Henry Ford Museum Archives, Dearborn, MI.

Stefaniuk, Myroslava. *Dibrova Diary*. Saline, MI: privately printed, 2018.

Stefaniuk, Myroslava, and Fred E. Dohrs. *Ukrainians of Detroit*. Detroit: Wayne State University, 1979.

Stefaniw, Stepan, Wolodymyr Pytlowanyj, and Dr. Nicholas Bartkiw. "Ukrainians in Flint." In *Ukrainians in Detroit and Michigan: Commemorating the Millennium of Christianity in Ukraine*. Detroit: Ukrainian Millennium Council, 1988.

Strazhnyk, Lyudmyla. "Easter in the USA: How Ukrainians from the Frankivsk Region Celebrate Easter Abroad." *Reporter*, April 29, 2016.

Subtelny, Orest. *Ukrainians in North America*. Toronto: University of Toronto Press, 1991.

Sullivan, Patricia. "Helen Petrauskas, 61; Ford's Top Safety Exec Promoted Air Bags." *Los Angeles Times*, March 13, 2006.

Suprun, Ulana. "One Hundred Days of Health Care Reform in Ukraine." *U.S. News and World Report*, December 22, 2016.

Sushko, Orest, dir. *Music of Survival: The Story of the Ukrainian Bandurist Chorus*. DVD. prod. Orest Sushko. Living Strings Productions, 2014.

Tarnowsky, Philemon. "The Ruthenians." *Immigrants in America Review*. New York: Committee for Immigrants in America, 1916.

"Thriving Local Ukrainian Community Turns Attention to Homeland." *Traverse City*

Record Eagle, May 9, 2015. https://www.record-eagle.com/.

Tymkiv, Bohdan, and Roksolana Tymkiv. "Sacral Wood Carving of Ukrainian Artists of the Western Diaspora." *Scientific Notes of Ostroh Academy,* ser. Historical Sciences (2015). https://journals.oa.edu.ua/Historical/article/view/1427.

"Ukrainian Embroidery." Textile Research Center. https://www.trc-leiden.nl/ trc-needles/regional-traditions/europe-and-north-america/embroideries/ ukrainian-embroidery.

"Ukrainians in Muskegon Heights." *Ukrainians in Detroit and Michigan: Commemorating the Millennium of Christianity in Ukraine.* Detroit: Ukrainian Millennium Council, 1988.

"Ukrainians in Saginaw." *Ukrainians in Detroit and Michigan: Commemorating the Millennium of Christianity in Ukraine.* Detroit: Ukrainian Millennium Council, 1988.

"United by Faith: Joint Pentecost Service Embraces Ukrainian, American Traditions." *Traverse City Record Eagle,* May 14, 2016.

United States Census Bureau, "Population Profile of the United States." U.S. Department of Commerce. http://www.census.gov/population/www/pop-profile/profile2000.html.

Werstman, Vladimir. *The Ukrainians in America, 1608–1975: A Chronology and Fact Book.* Dobbs Ferry, NY: Oceana, 1976.

Wichar, Nancy Karen. *Ukrainians of Metropolitan Detroit.* Chicago: Arcadia, 2009.

Wichorek, Michael, and Martha Wichorek. *Ukrainians in Detroit.* Detroit: privately printed, 1968.

Woodford, Frank B., and Arthur M. Woodford. *All Our Yesterdays: A Brief History of Detroit.* Detroit: Wayne State University Press, 1969.

Zakala, Andrij. "Ukrainians in Jackson." In *Ukrainians in Detroit and Michigan: Commemorating the Millennium of Christianity in Ukraine.* Detroit: Ukrainian Millennium Council, 1988.

Zunz, Olivier. *The Changing Face of Inequality: Urbanization, Industrial Development, and Immigrants in Detroit, 1880–1920.* Chicago: University of Chicago Press, 1982.

Index

87–89; in Plast, 54; in religion, 44, 65; in Ukrainian schools, 86–87; women's leadership in, 45

late fourth-wave and recent immigration, 23–24

Levitsky, Leo, 31

liquors, 73

Liskiwsky, Mykola, 112, 113

Liskiwsky, Olga, 88 (n.†), 113–15

M

mining, viii, 7, 61, 109

Muskegon Heights, 61, 67–68

mutual aid societies, 29, 42, 60; in Detroit, 39–42, 44, 60; in Flint, 66; in Jackson, 64

N

nativism, 10–11, 49

Nazis, 18, 19, 20; collaborating with, 125 (n. 74), 130 (n. 88); racial policy, 19

network lines, 4, 9, 10, 11, 17, 21, 23, 24, 27, 28, 60, 109; and immigration, 122 (n. 5)

O

OUN (Ukrainian Nationalist Home Army), 18, 19, 55, 125 (n. 68, 74); Fedorak's involvement with, 95

P

Panchuk, Ivan, 55, 63, 99–101, 129 (n. 74), 137 (n. 38)

parishes, in Detroit-Metro: in Flint, 66; in Grand Rapids, 64; Holy Trinity, 37; Immaculate Conception, 33, 35–36,

39, 51, 85, 86, 90, 127 (n. 43); Our Lady of Perpetual Help, 36–37; Saint Andrew, 39; Saint John the Baptist, 31, 33, 34, 35; Saint Josaphat, 35–36, 86, 90; Saint Mary Protectress, 37, 89; Saint Michael the Archangel, 36; Saints Peter and Paul, 32, 127 (n. 40); in Saginaw, 67

paska, 74, 75, 85–86

Petrauskas, Helen, 101–3

Petrykevich, Jaroslava Maria, 30, 44, 48, 49, 129 (n. 67)

Plast, 50, 54, 88, 110; at Dibrova, 53; and Mary V. Beck, 92

Putnam, Robert, 58–59, 110

pysanky, 53, 79, 80–81, 85

Pyskir, Maria Savchyn, 18, 19, 125 (n. 68)

R

rushnyky, 52

S

Saginaw, 61, 67; Saginaw Valley State. See also Seniuk

second-wave immigration, 10–17, 22, 23, 28, 29, 35, 39, 40, 42, 45, 46, 47, 50, 61, 66, 67, 127 (n. 26); in Flint, 66; in Saginaw, 67; traditional clothing, 71; Stefan Tymoshenko, 107; Stephen Wichar, 9

Seniuk, Roman, 81

Soroka, Solomia, 103, 111

Stefaniuk, Myroslava, 53, 103, 105

Stefansky, Mykola, vii, 3, 7, 26, 27, 28, 30, 121 (n. 2); first neighborhood, 31; first St. John's, 31, 35